THE FIRES OF JUBILEE

Books by Stephen B. Oates

William Faulkner: The Man and the Artist

Biography as High Adventure: Life-Writers Speak on Their Art

Abraham Lincoln: The Man Behind the Myths

THE CIVIL WAR QUARTET:

   Let the Trumpet Sound: The Life of Martin Luther King, Jr.

   With Malice Toward None: The Life of Abraham Lincoln

   The Fires of Jubilee: Nat Turner's Fierce Rebellion

   To Purge This Land with Blood: A Biography of John Brown

Our Fiery Trial

Portrait of America (2 volumes)

Visions of Glory

Rip Ford's Texas

Confederate Cavalry West of the River

Deep in the woods near Cabin Pond, Nat and his confederates work out their plans. From an old print published by J. D. Torrey, New York.

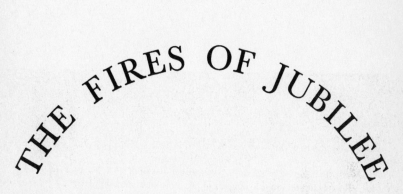

THE FIRES OF JUBILEE

Nat Turner's Fierce Rebellion

STEPHEN B. OATES

Perennial
An Imprint of HarperCollins*Publishers*

A hardcover edition of this book was published in 1975 by Harper & Row, Publishers.

THE FIRES OF JUBILEE. Copyright © 1975 by Stephen B. Oates. All rights reserved. Printed in the United States of America. No part of this book may be used or reproduced in any manner whatsoever without written permission except in the case of brief quotations embodied in critical articles and reviews. For information address HarperCollins Publishers Inc., 10 East 53rd Street, New York, NY 10022.

HarperCollins books may be purchased for educational, business, or sales promotional use. For information please write: Special Markets Department, HarperCollins Publishers Inc., 10 East 53rd Street, New York, NY 10022.

First HarperPerennial edition published 1990.

Reprinted in Perennial 2004.

The Library of Congress has catalogued the hardcover edition as follows:

Oates, Stephen B.
    The fires of jubilee.
    Includes bibliographical references and index.
    1. Turner, Nat, 1880?–1831.   2. Southampton
Insurrection, 1831.   I. Title.
F232.S7022   975.5'55'030924 [B]   74-1584
ISBN 0-06-013228-0

ISBN 0-06-091670-2 (pbk.)

07 LINO/RRD-H 50 49 48 47 46 45 44 43 42 41

For my mother and my father

CONTENTS

Foreword to the Perennial Library Edition

He is the most famous slave insurgent in American history, the victim of a violent system who struck back with retributive violence. His rebellion illustrates a profound truth. As Lerone Bennett says, "Nat Turner reminds us that oppression is a kind of violence which pays in coins of its own minting. He reminds us that the first and greatest of all gospels is this: that individuals and systems always reap what they sow."

When I wrote this biography of Nat, I tried to tell his story with empathy and accuracy. Through the technique of dramatic narration, I wanted to transport readers back to Nat's time so that they might suffer with him and see the world of slavery and the Old South through his eyes. That way they might gain melancholy insight into what it was like to be a slave. They might appreciate Nat for the complex, paradoxical figure he was, a man capable of love and hatred, doubt and thundering visions, sensitivity and messianic rage. They might understand why Nat finally chose the sword as his instrument of liberation, and why he set out to fulfill the injunction in Exodus that "thou shalt give life for life, eye for eye, tooth for tooth, hand for hand, foot for foot, burning for burning." By placing Nat and his revolt in proper historical context, I hoped to convey how the insurrection shocked the slave South to its foundations, exacerbated sectional tensions, and pointed the way to the Civil War thirty years later.

I also included an epilogue about my pilgrimage to Southampton County in 1973; in it, I sought to demonstrate that a good deal more goes into biography than reading documents and books in a library. The epilogue has an artistic purpose, too, for it attempts to show that past and present really are a continuum. In fact, the last scene of the epilogue circles back thematically to 1832 and reveals a sad truth about the durability of human prejudice. In 1832, a Virginia newspaper editor, in defending gradual emancipation and colonization over immediate manumission, argued that whites could not overcome their racial hostilities overnight. In the epilogue, I quoted a Virginia banker who said the same thing in 1973.

I also noted what little Virginia officialdom had then done to commemorate Nat's rebellion. Since 1973, things have gotten worse. The local historical marker about Nat described in the epilogue, a sign that once stood along Highway 58 in Southampton County, is no longer there. And the old homes that figured in the rebellion, the ones I visited in 1973 and wrote about in the epilogue, are gone as well. Clearly Nat Turner is not someone the local and state establishments want to remember. Yet Nat's spirit is still alive in Southampton County, in the legends and folklore of local blacks. I like to think that Nat also lives in *The Fires of Jubilee* and that this is one of the reasons the book has remained in print.

On the wall of my study, I keep a likeness of Nat, along with photographs of John Brown, Abraham Lincoln, and Martin Luther King, Jr.—the subjects of three of my other biographies. For me, the four lives are all of a piece: They form a biographical quartet centered around the greater Civil War era and its century-old legacies. All four of my subjects were driven, visionary men, all were absorbed in the issues of slavery and race, and all devised their own solutions to those inflammable problems. And all perished, too, in the conflicts and hostilities that have surrounded the quest for freedom and equality in this country. While *The Fires of Jubilee* can be read entirely on its own, it is part of a larger biographical design.

At this moment, I saw more clearly than ever the brutalizing effects of slavery upon both slave and slaveowner.

—FREDERICK DOUGLASS

If our work has any final value, that value must depend very largely on our ability to see the essential truth beyond the darkness and the error . . . to perform the historian's difficult task not only with the historian's competence but also with the skill, the insight and the demanding conscience of the literary artist.

—BRUCE CATTON

THE FIRES OF JUBILEE

PROLOGUE:
SOUTHAMPTON COUNTY, 1831

Some seventy miles below Richmond, in the southeastern part of Virginia along the North Carolina border, lay a little-known backwater called Southampton County. It was a rolling, densely forested area, with farms, plantations, and crossroad villages carved out of the woods. In 1831 most of the farms and smaller plantations were hardly distinguishable from one another—the houses were charmless, two-story rectangles, surrounded by haystacks and corn and cotton patches. Around the "big house" were various satellite sheds, a one-room kitchen, a barn, and maybe some slave cabins. Out in back were pungent outhouses poised on the edge of a slope or a steep ravine. A typical homestead had a menagerie of dogs, chickens, hogs, cows, mules, and maybe a couple of horses. And it had an apple orchard, too, for the succulent fruit not only commanded a fair price at market, but was the source of Southampton's most cherished product—an apple brandy potent enough to make a sailor reel. Not a homestead was complete without a brandy still, and the county's most popular citizens were those with well-stocked cellars.

The county seat or "county town" was Jerusalem, a smoky cluster of buildings where pigs rooted in the streets and old-timers spat tobacco juice in the shade of the courthouse. Consisting of some 175 souls, Jerusalem lay on the forested bank of the Nottoway River some fifty or sixty miles from Norfolk and the Atlantic Ocean. To the west of Jerusalem was Bethlehem Crossroads and to the southwest a loose cluster of homesteads called Cross Keys. Such villages were the nerve centers of Southampton's social life—here on Sundays and holidays white families gathered to hear preaching, dance to fiddles, enjoy a communal barbecue, joke, gossip, cheer on a shooting match or a horse race, get drunk, talk about the weather or argue about politics in their distinct Virginia accent ("hoose" for house). Most political discussions focused on local issues, for Southampton had no newspapers of its own and people here lived in considerable isolation from the outside world. What news they received came mainly from travelers and express riders, who brought mail in from Petersburg, Norfolk, and Murfreesboro down in North Carolina.

Although Southampton was a remote, generally lackluster neighborhood, it did have a planter class and in that respect was no different from most other Southern tidewater communities. If you had to own at least 20 slaves to rank as a planter, then 96 of Southampton's 734 slaveholders—about 13 percent—could claim that coveted distinction. Some fifteen men, with names like Newsom, Worrell, and Briggs, owned fifty slaves or more—which theoretically classified them as aristocrats. And Thomas Ridley, old man Urquhart, and John Kelly possessed large plantations with 145 to 179 Negroes apiece, which, in terms of slave wealth, placed *them* among the Old South's elite. Evidently these backwater squires had inherited or married into most of their possessions and had bought the rest. Some enterprising fellows had even constructed homes that were impressive by Southampton standards—with columned front porches and imported finery—and now found themselves hard-pressed to meet their mortgage payments. Still, Southampton's large planters lacked the tradition and prestige—and the majestic, landscaped mansions—that characterized Virginia's established gentry, especially the patricians along the great tidewater rivers in the more eastern and northeastern counties.

As was true of the rest of Dixie, most of Southampton's slaveowners resided on modest farms, some fighting to climb up the social and economic scale, others scratching out a hardscrabble existence from their crops and livestock. What is more, over one-third of Southampton's white families owned no slaves, none at all, and the

2

average for the entire county was ten or eleven per slaveowning family. Many small slaveholders could not afford overseers and worked alongside their Negroes in the orchards and cotton patches. Though Virginia was no longer in a depression in 1831, the state had suffered over the past decade, as soil exhaustion and ruinous farm prices—particularly in the early 1820s—had plagued farmers and planters alike. In Southampton, assessed land values had declined sharply during the last twenty years, and a number of whites had moved on to new cotton lands in Georgia and Alabama, so that the county's population was now almost 60 percent black, with some 6,500 whites and 9,500 Negroes residing there. While most of the blacks were still enslaved, an unusual number—some 1,745, in fact—were "free persons of color." Only three counties in all of tidewater Virginia had more free Negroes than that.[1]

By Southern white standards, enlightened benevolence did exist in Southampton County—and it existed in the rest of the state as well. Virginians liked to boast that slavery was not so harsh in the Old Dominion as it was on the brutal cotton plantations in the Deep South. Sure, Virginians conceded, there might be occasional mistreatment in the form of a sadistic overseer or a licentious poor white who hankered after slave girls, but respectable Virginians convinced themselves that all was sweetness and sunshine in their master-slave relations. Why, on Sundays Virginia masters even took their darkies to white churches, where they got to sit at the back or up in the balcony, murmuring a rehearsed *"Amen"* from time to time. After church, the slaves often gathered in a field—a shack or a shed—to conduct their own praise meetings, to shout and sing in an arcane language that aroused little interest among picnicking whites, who dismissed the noise as innocuous "nigger gabble."

Southampton whites, too, were pretty lax toward their slaves, allowing them to gather for religious purposes, visit other farms, and even travel to Jerusalem on market Saturdays to see relatives and friends. After all, what was there to worry about? Southampton's slaves were well treated, whites said, and apart from a few solitary incidents the county had never had any severe slave troubles. True, the Negroes did get a bit carried away in their praise meetings these days, with much too much clapping and singing. And true, some white evangelists were coming in from outside the county and "ranting" about equality at local revivals. But generally things were quiet and unchanged in this tidewater neighborhood, where time seemed to stand as still as a windless summer day.[2]

But all was not so serene as whites liked to believe. For a storm was brewing in Southampton's backwoods, in the slave cabins northwest of Cross Keys. It blew up with shattering suddenness, an explosion of black rage that struck Southampton County like a tornado roaring out of the Southern night. In the early morning hours of August 22, 1831, a band of slave insurgents, led by a black mystic called Nat Turner, burst out of the forests with guns and axes, plunging southeastern Virginia—and much of the rest of the South —into convulsions of fear and racial violence. It turned out to be the bloodiest slave revolt in Southern history, one that was to have a profound and irrevocable impact on the destinies of Southern whites and blacks alike.

Part One

THIS INFERNAL SPIRIT
OF SLAVERY

Southampton County early in the 1800s . . .

He was living in the innocent season of his life, in those carefree years before the working age of twelve when a slave boy could romp and run about the plantation with uninhibited glee. Clad only in a "tow" shirt which hung about his knees, Nat and the other children—white and black alike—played together like prattling sparrows, oblivious to that future time when white adults would permanently separate them, sending the white children to schools or tutors and the blacks to the fields, dividing them for the rest of their lives into free and chattel—into the blessed and the wretched of their Christian world. But for now, in these innocent years, the children frolicked and fraternized in democratic abandon.

Nat was especially close to John Clark Turner, who was one of the Master's three sons and about his age. Sometimes little Nathaniel Francis came over from a neighboring plantation, and the three boys raided melon patches, collected little-boy treasures, and explored the thick forests about the Turner place, with their macabre shadows and cawing birds. They swam and fished in ponds there and set out traps for coon and possum. They might also visit the carpenter's shed, where skilled slaves fashioned cabinets and chairs for the Big House, or play mumblety-peg near the brandy still, where other blacks transformed fermented apple juice into brandy for the Master's table. Nat and John Clark also received the same religious instruction, since the Turners—Benjamin and Elizabeth—were Methodists who sought to instill Christian beliefs and righteousness in their thirty-odd slaves.

So Nat in his young years cavorted about the home place as slave children did generally in Virginia. He took his meals in the Negro cabins—meals of corn mush and bacon fat which he ate out of wooden bowls with a slave-carved spoon. His daytime supervisor was his grandmother, Old Bridget, an aged and wrinkled woman—too old to work any more—who regaled the boy with slave tales and stories from the Bible. Nat had become very attached to his grandmother, for she praised him and helped teach him the same prayers the Master and Mistress had taught to her.[1]

A word about the Turners. Benjamin, getting along in years now, owned a modest plantation—a large farm really—of several hundred acres on Rosa Swamp, in a remote neighborhood "down county" from Jerusalem. Benjamin belonged to the third generation of a large Turner family, who had migrated to southeastern Virginia back in the eighteenth century, and he had acquired his holdings through inheritance, marriage, and additional purchases. But his land was so heavily forested that only about one hundred acres were under cultivation. He raised a little tobacco, and more corn and apples than cotton. His two-story house was large enough to accommodate overnight guests, and in his cellar and sheds were enough barrels to hold 1,500 gallons of apple brandy. No doubt his brandy supply was one of the main reasons why horseback Methodist preachers, traveling the Jerusalem-Murfreesboro road, liked to come over to Turner's place and stay the night with a fellow Methodist.[2]

The Turners had become Methodists back in the late 1780s or early 1790s when the church was in its infancy. In 1784, a year after the Revolution, the Methodists had broken away from the Anglican Church, or Church of England, and had established the Methodist Episcopal Church of America, with Francis Asbury as its first bishop and most indefatigable circuit rider. Traditionally the Turner family had been Anglicans, but after the Revolution Benjamin and Elizabeth wanted to escape the British stigma and switched to Methodism. Like scores of other striving, acquisitive Americans, the Turners were very much attracted to Methodist doctrine, with its emphasis on free will and individual salvation, and to the church's irrepressible missionary zeal. The Turners became prominent church folk in their community and did all they could to spread the faith, holding Methodist services in the neighborhood chapel and traveling for miles to hear one of Asbury's pulpit-banging preachers. For these were the years when Methodist evangelists, out to save America from Satan and to build a mighty church for themselves, rode across Virginia, North Carolina, Tennessee, and Kentucky, presenting Methodism in a smoking, earthy language few people could resist. By 1801 frenzied camp meetings lit up the Southern backwoods, as Methodists, Baptists, and maverick Presbyterians all joined in the evangelical crusade against godlessness.

In those early years of the Republic, Methodist revivalists also inveighed against the evil of slaveowning, though they were hardly the first sect to do so. On the contrary, the redoubtable Quakers had been foes of slavery since the colonial period, especially in Virginia and North Carolina. After the Revolution, North Carolina Quakers were so outspoken against the institution that a grand jury accused them of planting "dangerous" notions in the slaves that might incite them to violence. The Quakers replied that it was not their pronouncements but the slave system itself that caused Negro unrest. That, of course, only got them branded as "agitators" in North Carolina, but they went right on denouncing slavery nonetheless.

In the 1780s the Methodists also attacked the institution, contending in conference and church alike that human bondage was "contrary to the laws of God and hurtful to society." So antislavery were the early Methodists that Francis Asbury visited the South on several occasions, both to convert sinners and to speak against slaveholding. After a Methodist meeting in one Virginia county, Asbury talked with "some select friends about slavekeeping, but they could not bear it; this I know, God will plead the cause of the oppressed, though it gives offense to say so here. O Lord, banish the infernal spirit of slavery from thy dear Zion."

The Methodists, Quakers, and antislavery Baptists made some whites feel guilty enough to liberate their slaves, especially in backwater Southampton County where a number of "free coloreds" began to appear. But most Southern whites were not about to emancipate their Negroes, because slave ownership was not only a tremendous status symbol in the Old South, but was the most tried and tested means of racial control in their white supremacist society. Southern whites might pray that God forgive their lesser sins (profligacy and drunkenness) and might even succumb to the "holy jerks" and howl like dogs at some fire-and-brimstone revival. But no church could ever scare them into wholesale emancipation, into unleashing all the hundreds of thousands of slaves in Dixie, because in Southern white minds that would bring about social chaos and racial catastrophe. By 1800, Asbury and his Methodist colleagues, confronted with growing hostility and intransigence on the part of Southern whites of all classes, had surrendered to the doctrine of necessity and accommodated the church to slavery where it legally existed. After all, if the Methodists were going to make theirs a potent church in the United States, they could not afford to alienate the South, where Methodism drew so much of its strength. Still regarding bondage as an evil, the church did restrict slaveholding among its ministry and did prohibit members from buying and selling slaves (but not from owning them). Subsequently the Methodists softened even the injunction against trading in slaves; most Southern members ignored it anyway. By 1804 the church as a whole had given up on complete emancipation—for that was impossible in the South—and had settled for saving the souls of "the poor Africans" by converting them to Christianity. A Methodist ordinance of that year even advised that preachers "admonish and exhort all slaves to render due respect and obedience" to the commands of their masters. . . .[3]

Perhaps Benjamin Turner felt a pang of remorse about owning Negroes—but not enough to manumit them as some of his neighbors had done. No doubt he and Elizabeth both rested more easily when their church stopped trying to eradicate the peculiar institution and set about Christianizing the slaves for a better time ahead. So that their own Negroes might be saved, the Turners held prayer services on their farm and took the blacks to Sunday chapel.

Among such slaves were Nat's grandmother and his mother, Nancy. According to black and white tradition, Nancy was a large, spirited, olive-skinned young African, one of 400,000 native Africans imported to North America before 1808, to toil as bondsmen on farms and plantations there. While most of these people came from the agrarian tribes of West Africa, Nancy's home was supposed to have been in the North's Nile River country. If folk chroniclers are correct, then slave raiders or warlike natives abducted Nancy when she was in her late teens and marched her hundreds of miles to the coast. Eventually she fell into the hands of European traders, who branded the girl and herded her aboard a crowded slave ship bound for the New World. She too endured the horrors of the "middle passage," crammed into a small hold with a hundred other chained and manacled Africans, many of them convinced that the white skins planned to boil and eat them. Why else were they here? Why else were they in chains? Driven to madness in the rancid, claustrophobic bowels of the slave ships, many Africans maimed themselves, committed suicide. Others starved to death or died of some white man's disease. If the Africans somehow survived the Atlantic passage, the slave ships disgorged them into some fly-infested slave pen in the New World—on Cuba or Santo Domingo, in the British West Indies, Brazil, Mexico, or the new Republic of the United States.

Storytellers claim that Nancy landed at Norfolk in 1795, when a terrible insurrection was raging down on the French island of Santo Domingo in the Caribbean. White traders then drove her inland on a slave coffle, exhibiting her on various auction blocks along the way. Sometime in 1799 Benjamin Turner bought her at a slave sale, took her home, and christened her Nancy. To the Turners, of course, she seemed a wild heathen (they knew nothing about African manners, religion, language), though smart enough to make a good slave if she could be tamed and Christianized. Soon after her arrival at the Turner place she married one of Old Bridget's sons, whose name is not known. On October 2, 1800, Nancy gave birth to Nat, or Nathaniel, which in Hebrew meant "the gift of God." Tradition has it that Nancy tried to kill the baby rather than see him raised a slave and that she had to be tied up for a while. In time she submitted to slavery—there was little else she could do—and learned to speak English. It is possible that she went on to become a house servant and so one of the slave elite.[4]

By the time Nat was four or five years old, Nancy was extremely proud of him. Bright-eyed and quick to learn, he was a fine one. He stood out among the other children. Once Nancy overheard him telling his playmates about some event that had happened before he was born. How could he know about that? Nancy asked. Had somebody told him? No, the boy replied, somehow he just knew. Entranced, Nancy fetched other slaves to hear. Yes, they agreed, he described the episode just as it happened; he certainly did. They were "greatly astonished," Nat recalled later, and remarked that only the Almighty could have given him such powers of recollection.

After that, his mother and father both praised him for his brilliance and extraordinary imagination. Both made him thrill with self-esteem. They showed the other slaves how Nat had congenital bumps and scars on his head and chest. African tradition held that a male with markings like these was destined to become a leader. Did they need any more proof? Could there be any doubt about the boy's future? And Nat's parents, his grandmother, and the other Turner slaves all agreed that he was "intended for some great purpose," that Nat would surely become a prophet.

One day the precocious boy astonished them even more. To stop him from crying, one of the slaves gave him a book from the Big House to play with. Nat proceeded to spell out the names of objects in the volume. How could he *do* these things? Did he not possess amazing supernatural powers? It is doubtful that his parents could read or write, as some chroniclers have claimed, so who taught Nat his letters remains a mystery. All he remembered was that he started reading and writing with remarkable ease—a gift that made him "a source of wonder" around the Turner neighborhood. After all, a literate slave was not all that common in the Old South, even in Virginia. Another black observed that a slave who could read a book and write his name was "a very important fellow" in any slave quarters.

Nat was certainly an important fellow among his playmates, who wanted to apply some of his brilliance to their pranks. With a genius like Nat to lead them, think of the successes they would enjoy! Think of the cakes they could steal, the brandy they could filch, the traps they could sabotage in the forests! Well, Nat agreed to plan their roguery—frankly he was flattered—but he now refused to steal anything himself. Pilfering, after all, did not become a future prophet. He never touched liquor either. And he never swore, never played practical jokes, and never cared a thing for white people's money. All of which made him more mysterious than ever in the eyes of children and adults alike.

Nat's superior intelligence did not escape Master Benjamin's notice. Being a Methodist, the old Master not only approved of Nat's literacy but encouraged him to study the Bible. He began taking the boy to prayer meetings, where he sat at the back of the chapel with the other slaves. Proud of his bright slave boy, Benjamin showed him off to his guests—especially those tired and thirsty itinerate preachers who came to share his table and his brandy. Well, the preachers were infatuated with this little darky who could read books and recite his prayers. And they and everybody else in the boy's world—his parents, grandmother, and Master Benjamin—all remarked that he had too much sense to be raised in bondage, that he "would never be of any service to anyone as a slave."[5]

The seasons of Nat's life changed in a succession of unexpected shocks, as confused and bewildering as windswept leaves. The first shock came when his father ran away from the Turner place and escaped to the North. Nobody knows why he left beyond an innate and unquenchable longing to break out of slavery, even at the cost of losing his wife and son. So Nat's father was gone, never to be seen again in Southampton County. Yet Nat never forgot him.[6]

Another jolt came in 1809, when the boy was nine years old. In that year, Samuel Turner—the Master's oldest son—bought some 360 acres from his father for a nominal sum. Located just two miles south of the home place, Samuel's land used to be the old Kindred plantation. Of course, Samuel needed slaves to work his cotton patches, so Benjamin loaned him eight of his own—Nat and his mother among them. And so the boy left the plantation of his birth and went to stay with Master Samuel, a young bachelor.

In October, 1810, Master Benjamin died in the wake of a typhoid epidemic that swept through the neighborhood. Not long after old Benjamin had been buried in the family graveyard, Elizabeth also took ill and died. In his will, Benjamin broke up the home estate, dividing his land and slaves among the children. Now Nat, Nancy, and Old Bridget all became the legal property of Master Samuel.

Samuel was then in his mid-twenties, a man of immense piety and rectitude. Shortly before his father had died, the old man had donated an acre of land on which to raise a Methodist church, a backwoods cathedral to be called Turner's Meeting House. Young Samuel not only helped build and organize the church but became an elder. He seldom missed a Sunday service unless he was too sick to walk. And he took his slaves along so that they might learn something about Christian obedience.

From all appearances, Samuel was a harder taskmaster than his father had been, and like many another slaveowner in the Old South, he understood that Christianity could be used not merely to save heathen souls, but to keep the slaves from striking back or running off as Nat's father had done. So at prayer meetings Samuel Turner and his fellow churchmen rehearsed for the blacks a number of carefully selected Bible lessons which God intended them to follow: If they did not obey their masters and perform their allotted tasks, God would burn them in the flames of an eternal Hell. The Bible said that God wanted Negroes to be the white man's slaves, that this was their proper station in life. One must not question the wisdom of the Almighty. And He would become furious if they were impudent, sassy, or sullen, and would punish them terribly at Judgment Day. And the slaves must beware of Satan—that cunning, wicked master of Hell—for it was Satan who created their desires for freedom and tempted them to run away. To be good children of the Lord, the slaves must accept their lot, be meek and faithful, patient and submissive, even if their masters were cruel. They must never resist even the most vicious master. Leave it to the Lord to punish him. Only the Lord knows what is best. "You either deserve correction, or you do not deserve it," white preachers warned the slaves. "But whether you deserve it or not, it is your duty; and the Almighty God requires, that you bear it patiently." And if you do, God "will reward you in heaven, and the punishment you suffer here shall turn to your exceedingly great glory hereafter." After such sermons, white masters told their slaves how lucky they were to be here rather than in "dark and benighted Africa." For in America they could hear the sound of the gospel and receive the true faith.[7]

Such religious instruction reflected a growing malaise about slavery in Virginia's white community, and a literate, God-fearing man like

Samuel Turner certainly shared in that uneasiness. He traveled to Jerusalem on market Saturdays. He heard the talk around the courthouse and post office. He saw the communiqués which express riders brought in from Richmond and other towns. For years now, ever since the 1790s, slave discontent had seemed on the rise in both the Old Dominion and many other parts of the South. Stories circulated about increasing slave disaffection and vandalism—about marauding Negro outlaws who hid in the swamps by day and raided farms and plantations by night. There were accounts, too, of suspicious fires in various communities across the South—a blazing barn here, a burning haystack there—which whites almost always blamed on slaves. Worse, there were guarded reports of actual revolts and insurrection plots in Richmond, Norfolk, and other towns in North and South Carolina—occurrences that whites always tried to veil in secrecy. "It is a subject not to be mentioned," a lady wrote a friend about an insurrection plot in South Carolina, and she cautioned her friend "to say nothing about it," nothing at all.

From the very beginning of slavery in the seventeenth century, Southern whites had taken precautions against insurrections and had inflicted brutal punishment on rebellious Negroes. In 1767, after several overseers were mysteriously slain near Alexandria, Virginia, whites there decapitated four accused slaves and placed their "grinning skulls" on chimneys as a warning to other blacks. Such savage white reprisals occurred more than once in the colonial South. But apart from a few isolated episodes, no legitimate slave revolts broke out in colonial America. Indeed, before the birth of the Republic most slave resistance took the form of individual acts of vandalism, sabotage, or escape.

Then came the 1790s, when a full-scale slave rebellion rocked the French island of Santo Domingo. The fighting was unspeakably savage, with whites and blacks slaughtering one another in a carnage of racial violence that ultimately cost some sixty thousand lives. When the insurgents smashed all French resistance and established an independent Haiti, the first black republic in the New World, Southern whites were plagued with anxieties. *Can it happen here? What if it happens here?*

Some thought it was already happening here, for rumors of slave rebelliousness rippled across the South in the wake of Santo Domingo, and whites desperately feared that the insurrection fever had spread to America as well. The slave grapevine—an elaborate oral communications system that spread news throughout the slave community—hummed with accounts of war and resistance in the New World; and many whites who overheard their servants no doubt mistook a guarded whisper for some sinister design.[8] And in 1799— the very year old Benjamin Turner bought Nancy—backwater Southampton County experienced its first serious slave trouble. It happened when white drivers brought a slave coffle from Maryland through the county, bound for Georgia. Without warning, some of these desperate Negroes "rose up" and killed two whites. Labeling this a revolt, county authorities convicted and hanged four of the slaves. Some whites blamed this and other "outrages" in Virginia on the Santo Domingo virus—a sickness, whites believed, that arrived on slave ships from the West Indies, infected American slaves, and caused them to run away or murder people in their delirium.[9]

Then in 1800—the year Thomas Jefferson ran for the Presidency and the year Nat Turner was born—whites uncovered the Gabriel Prosser conspiracy in Richmond, the first large-scale insurrection plot the South had known up to that time. The leaders were chiefly skilled urban slaves who had become highly politicized by the rhetoric of the American and French revolutions—by the enlightened ideal that all men were born equal, that all enjoyed the inalienable rights of life, liberty, and the pursuit of happiness and had a natural right to rebel when those rights were denied. So stated America's cherished Declaration of Independence, yet somehow its noble principles applied only to white people and not to Negroes. Gabriel and his friends were enraged at such hypocrisy, enraged that the United States should institutionalize slavery and yet proclaim itself the freest and most enlightened republic in the world, enraged that Negroes should be arbitrarily chained to the gutters of the American system just because they had black skins. Well, then, they would rise up against the system: away with it in an inferno of smoke and fire. They attended black religious meetings in and about Richmond, where Gabriel's brother—a black preacher—told the plantation slaves about "the days of old when the Israelites were in service to King Pharaoh" and about how Moses had broken their bonds and led them to freedom. But mostly the conspirators justified rebellion in political terms, arguing that "we have as much right to fight for our liberty as any men." Gabriel himself, an articulate blacksmith who stood six feet, two inches tall, exhorted his fellow blacks to stand and fight like men and vowed to fashion a silk flag emblazoned with *"death or liberty."* But theirs was not to be a war of aimless vengeance. They intended to spare Quakers, Methodists, and Frenchmen —for they had opposed slavery—and to fight only those who supported and governed the slave regime. Their plans called for Gabriel and his immediate followers to burn Richmond and take hostages like Governor James Monroe, a onetime revolutionary, whereupon slaves from the outlying plantations were to rise en masse. After that plans were flexible, allowing Gabriel to negotiate with the whites if that seemed feasible.

But the plantation slaves never gave him their complete support, and the conspiracy all but disintegrated in a vortex of confusion, betrayals, and violent weather. Warned by Negro informers what Gabriel was plotting, white authorities mobilized Richmond, alerted the state militia, and arrested Gabriel and his lieutenants before they could fire a shot. Resolved to say nothing about their work, Gabriel and some thirty-four collaborators went to the gallows in silence.

Though not a single white had died, the Gabriel conspiracy shook Virginians with volcanic fury, because it seemed incontestable proof that a Santo Domingo had been boiling right underneath them. Monroe wrote Jefferson that it was "unquestionably the most serious and formidable conspiracy we have ever known of the kind" and conceded that he had kept it a secret for as long as he dared. John Randolph, who saw the Negroes in prison, warned grimly: "The accused have exhibited a spirit, which, if it becomes general, must deluge the Southern country in blood. They manifested a sense of their rights, and contempt of danger, and a thirst for revenge which portend the most unhappy consequences." How to prevent the consequences? How to avoid a more lethal explosion? In Richmond, authorities established a public guard to police the blacks and protect the city. And there was a rising clamor in Virginia in favor of removing the free Negroes, whom many whites blamed for slave disturbances, and the Virginia legislature, meeting behind closed doors in secret deliberations, actually adopted resolutions that "obnoxious and dangerous" blacks be colonized outside the state. But the colonization movement floundered for lack of money, wide popular support, and consistent and creative planning—the same obstacles that later hindered the American Colonization Society. Meanwhile, to keep the slaves subdued, other Virginians advocated that a stronger militia system be devised, along with stringent enforcement of the slave codes and the elimination of the international slave trade (which Congress was to do in 1807–1808) so as to keep out rebellious Africans.[10]

For Southern whites, Santo Domingo and Gabriel Prosser left a searing legacy—a fear of slave uprisings that would haunt them for decades to come. In their minds, it became a dreadful word, *insurrection,* one that triggered nightmarish visions of death and destruction, of ax-wielding blacks—their once submissive "darkies" satanically transformed into powerful Gabriel Prossers or Haitian rebels—who butchered, burned, and raped their way across the South in an apocalypse of violence worse than Hell itself. That is why unexpected church bells now frightened whites so. That is why a haystack blazing against the night sky (a signal for the slaves to revolt?) seemed to many Southerners a harbinger of some unutterable doom. For should the slaves rise up and take over, what would happen to white women? To the white race? To Christianity? To civilization?

After 1800, with whites tightening up slave discipline, Negro discontent seemed to subside. But during the War of 1812 white fears started mounting again, and rumors swept the Southern states that the slaves might revolt and join the British. In truth, there was talk along the slave grapevine that British victory might result in Negro emancipation. But neither Britain nor the United States won the war—it ended in stalemate—and no slave insurrection broke out either. Nevertheless, many Virginians remained concerned about "our internal foe" and cautioned masters not to relax their controls over "the more dangerous internal population."[11]

But other Virginians contended that the vast majority of slaves now seemed passive and humble—the result of strict religious teachings mixed with enlightened supervision. In fact, if some whites advocated stricter slave laws to prevent insurrection, others argued that discipline ought to be tempered with some permissiveness. Yes, that was the best way to control the darkies—through enlightened benevolence (with a militia force to back it up). That and constant reassurances that the Gabriel business was only an aberration—a mistake of history—and would never happen again. Yet to make sure of that, you must give your slaves only censored sermons—and absolutely forbid them to talk with a Quaker or learn about Thomas Paine or Jefferson's Declaration. In fact, enlightened slaveowner or not, it was best to remove such writings from your library and go about your affairs with confidence and equanimity—much as Samuel Turner was doing down in Southampton County—so that your slaves would never suspect that you were anxious in any way.

Yes, that was the posture many slaveholders adopted in the years after Gabriel Prosser: let us believe that what we fear is not really to be feared, that what has happened did not actually happen, and that slavery—the source of all our dreary agonies that are not really agonies—is a necessary evil which we do not want but cannot remove. In truth, most Southerners preferred not to discuss the slavery problem; but if they did—to some congenial and sympathetic traveler, for example—they tended to apologize for the institution, as though it were an ugly family heirloom left to them by some sadistic relative. They blamed this "necessary evil" not on themselves, but on European slave traders who brought all those blacks to America in the first place, to the North as well as the South. After the Revolution, Southerners contended, they had become stuck with the institution, as the Northern states eradicated it by law, constitution, or court decree. Southerners insisted that they did not *like* slavery, but what could they do? They could not free their darkies as the Yankees had done. With so few blacks in relation to their white population, the Northern states could afford to liberate their small percentage of Negroes—what did they have to lose? But it was different with Southerners, what with their heavy concentration of blacks (some places they even outnumbered white people) and their correspondingly large investments. After the invention of the cotton gin in 1793, slavery became "an economic necessity," that everready excuse for slaveholders who felt embarrassed about the discrepancy between Jeffersonian idealism and human bondage, but could not bring themselves to do anything about it. So, no, most would rather not talk about any moral contradictions inherent in slavery in America . . . and anyway in their view they were concerned with something a lot more basic than contradictions: they were concerned about their survival. The survival of their white, Christian way of life. So they hushed up talk about the unspeakable (what the darky did in Richmond) and got on with their business of growing and selling cotton, corn, and tobacco, and tried to accept slavery as the will of Almighty God and to let God Himself take care of the problem in His own due time. . . .[12]

So went the catechism for farmers like Samuel Turner of Southampton County: accept the way things are, endure life's adversities, discipline slaves like children, go to chapel, work hard, count your blessings, plan for the future, be a success in your community, preserve and honor the family name.

Though a diligent farmer, Samuel did not yet own so much land or so many slaves as his father, but he did possess a two-story, eight-room manor house and was proud of it. Still, it was a lonely place without a wife and children—something all good Christian men should have. Soon one Elizabeth Williamson caught his eye: they courted at church picnics and barbecues, picked berries, visited Jerusalem, and eventually married.[13]

Meanwhile young Nat suffered the worst blow yet to his crumbling little-boy's world. As though Master Samuel's stern preachments were not bad enough, Nat now reached the age of twelve when slaves must go to work. Despite the boy's intelligence, Samuel did not appreciate his potential as a skilled slave and sent him out to the cotton patches with a half-dozen other field hands.

Going to work was more than Nat's final break with childhood. It also ended his democratic frolicking with white children, who went away to schools and academies while he was driven to the fields. Aware now of their separate and superior destinies, the whites no longer mixed with "nigger" kids like Nat, no longer romped and wrestled with them, fished and swam with them, ate watermelons and played with them. Now the white children ordered the "nigger" kids about, and set out to learn their proper roles as members of God's master class—a class they must strive with all their might to preserve and perpetuate. So their parents, teachers, ministers, and politicians told them over and over, until they embraced their superiority over Negroes as God's law, as the truth of truths.

So it was a rude awakening for Nat, just as it was for many other slave children who passed through that traumatic time: the first anguished recognition that *I am a slave. It's not just a word any more. I am really a slave, a piece of property, to be worked and ordered around like a mule.* For Nat it was an especially painful time, for he had been led to believe he might be freed one day. Had not everybody on Master Benjamin's place implied that he would be liberated because he was so smart? If so, then why was he being treated like an ordinary field hand—like Sam, Drew, Miver, and Elick, not one of whom could read and write, brag of special bumps and markings, or tell of things that happened before their births.[14]

And so began a dispiriting new season of Nat's life. He now rose before first light, ate a breakfast of cornpone and mush, milked the cows and fed the hogs and chickens. Then at daybreak there came the haunting bellow of a horn, ordering him and the other hands to the fields, to work there until dusk. They spent March and April planting cotton. In the summer, as the plants sprouted in Southampton's lackluster soil, as gray as gunpowder, the slaves hoed and grubbed in the fields, battling squadrons of mosquitoes and gnats as they moved. All about them were the swampy forests, moving against a background of thunderheads. The woods seemed to wall in the meadows and fields, giving them an air of solitude and remoteness from all the world beyond.

At high sun Nat and the other hands stopped for dinner: a bite of meal, maybe some bacon fat or salt pork, brought with them from the cabins. For a while they could nap or talk and sing together. Then Master Samuel or some hired driver would prod them, "Tumble up! Tumble up! Back to work with you." And so they passed the afternoons and evenings as they had the mornings. They picked worms off the cotton plants and then sowed corn and some tobacco in contiguous fields. Then they hoed these, too, singing all the while those spirituals that helped them endure their unendurable lives.

They sang to their hoes, to the cotton leaves, the plows, the mules and oxen. And they sang in the quiet dust of the evening, on the way back to their unowned, shipwreck homes. They sang about the sorrow and sadness—the hopes and aspirations—of their lives under the lash: they sang about Moses warring in evil lands, about God smiting sinners and commanding them, "Let my people go." They sang of broken families, of whippings, of revenge against the white man. And they sang of better times ahead, when all would be gladness in the kingdom.

> *No more rain fall for to wet you, Hallelujah,*
> *No more sun shine for to burn you,*
> *Dere's no hard trials*
> *Dere's no whips a-crackin'*
> *No evil-doers in de kingdom*
> *All is gladness in de kingdom.*

So young Nat toiled through the days, observing all, forgetting nothing, as he wielded his clumsy hoe. In August the slaves stripped the tobacco leaves from the stalks and bundled them to dry. When a thunderstorm lashed the countryside, they labored in the shacks and sheds, fixing broken tools, helping the women or the skilled slaves. In September or October, the cotton leaves ripened and fell away from the bolls, transforming the fields into oceans of white. Now it was picking time—the blacks moving like slow freighters through a cotton sea. They picked until their shoulders and fingers ached to the bones, for they must gather the bolls before the frosts came. When that was done, they had to harvest the corn, too, and pull and stack the hay. In between planting and harvesting the crops, they repaired fences, cleared new fields, chopped firewood, and did a variety of other chores. Then in the spring the cycle started again, a monotonous, mind-killing cycle that measured the tick-tock passing of their lives. And so "the human cattle" moved, recalled Frederick Douglass, a former slave, "hurried on by no hope of reward, no sense of gratitude . . . no prospect of bettering their condition; nothing, save the dread and terror of the slave-driver's lash. So goes one day, and so comes and goes another."

Still, not all slave life was bleak despair. At night, in their one-room cabins, the blacks could enjoy some respite from the white man's whip and rules. Gathered around the fireplace, the cabin scented with burning wood, they could tell stories to their children, listen to their woes, comfort and discipline them as best they knew. They ate their meager suppers on a box-crate table, sitting on chairs of sticks and vine. Afterward a wife could care for her husband, rubbing his muscles, tending to his blisters and sores. Or they could visit with slaves from next-door cabins, sing some songs, fashion homemade banjos, or speak in guarded tones of the latest news on the slave grapevine: an insurrection scare up in Petersburg, another in Louisiana. And then at last, when all the lanterns were out, when all was quiet except for the slow moan of the wind outside, a man and a woman could make love on their gunnysack bed, bound together in the intimacies of the night.

On Sundays, after the white man's services, slaves generally held their own praise meetings, their own dances and picnics. If their masters were tolerant, some slaves got to work their own garden patches, raising collards, peas, and sweet potatoes for special meals. Some might harvest enough to sell at market up in Jerusalem and bring in a few pennies of their own. Over the year a frugal man might save enough to buy whiskey for one of the holidays.

A prudent master, of course, gave his slaves holidays so they could let off steam. These usually included four days at Christmas, a week off after the crops were harvested, a day off on Easter and another off on the Fourth of July. For slaves a holiday was a marvelous affair—a time when you could let yourself go and get roaring drunk on whatever liquor was available. You were *supposed* to get drunk on holidays, a former slave declared, and if you didn't it was disgraceful. After harvest time, the master himself might throw an immense barbecue for his slaves—and even invite their relatives and friends from neighboring farms and plantations. Or the blacks simply held their own frolics: they wrestled, boxed, ran races, and yelled at rooster fights. And then they danced, often late into the holiday night, moving and clapping to the music of fiddles, banjos, whistles, tambourines, wooden clarinets, and drums—instruments used by their African forebears in similar singsong festivals. One of the more popular dances was "patting juba"—a complicated movement in which the slaves stamped their feet, clapped their hands, and patted their knees and chests, all in perfect rhythm to the beat of the music. And sometimes their songs turned on humorous and ironic themes, such as the one about Harper's Creek and roaring river:

> *Harper's creek and roaring ribber,*
> *Thar, my dear, we'll live forebber,*
> *Den we'll go to de Ingin Nation,*
> *All I want in dis creation,*
> *Is a pretty little wife and a big plantation.*

In the midst of such merriment, slave young people met and courted, some of them stealing off to make love somewhere. And so it went through the seasons—a few moments alone, away from the fields and meetings, away from the older people both black and white, when the young might glory in the discovery of one another, in all the suffering and uncertainty, pleasure and tenderness, of courtship and sexual love. And if there was a bond between them, whether they had already made love or wanted to for the first time, a slave couple usually married: first they got the master's permission (which was all they needed, since slave marriages were never legally sanctioned in the white man's South), and the master usually encouraged such unions, because they provided both discipline and stability in his slave quarters. Then the couple went to their cabin and "jumped over the broomstick" into their marriage bed. In time they would have children, but since both parents had to work, the children would grow up in a slave nursery supervised by aging slave women. But no matter how painful and limited family life could be, threatened as it was by the fear of being broken up in bad times and "sold off to Georgia," slaves nevertheless found in their families another slim bond that helped them endure.[15]

As it went on farms and plantations across Virginia and the Carolinas, so it went on Samuel Turner's farm in tidewater Southampton County. Here too the slaves found in family life and holidays a marginal way to enjoy themselves, take the edge off despair, salvage traditional folk customs. Young Nat, however, rarely participated in their leisure-time amusements—and never in the drinking. A brooding, introspective youth, he preferred to spend his spare time either in prayer or in improving his knowledge. He experimented in making gunpowder and exploited every opportunity to read books. When Master Samuel hired a tutor to instruct his children, Nat found ways to look at their histories and geographies. And he discovered in those books, he claimed, many things "that the fertility of my own imagination had depicted to me before."[16]

Still, it was religion that occupied Nat the most. At Negro praise meetings, he listened transfixed as black exhorters preached a different version of Christianity from what the white man offered, an alternate version that condemned slavery and fueled resistance to it. This was black religion—an amalgam of African mythology and Christian doctrines as slaves interpreted them, a unique religion that embodied the essence of the slaves' lives—their frustrations and sorrows, their memories, and their fantasies about a future world without whips and masters. An inquisitive youth, "observant of everything that was passing," Nat was quick to discern the power of the black preacher, who delivered his Bible sermons with stabbing gestures, singing out in a rhythmic language that was charged with emotion and vivid imagery. He was an acknowledged leader—a sacred leader—who through his trembling expressions, his cadences, inflections, and body movements articulated the deepest needs and feelings of his congregation. And the slaves, swept along by his magic, hummed and swayed in constant motion, punctuating his exhortation with *"Amen"* and *"Hallelujah,"* with *"Tell it to them, preacher."* And then all joined in a moving spiritual, "O my Lord delivered Daniel," clapping, clapping, "O why not deliver me." Until the power of the music, the clapping and shouting, drove old and young alike into "a frenzy of religious fervor."

There can be no doubt that the slave church (now a forest clearing, now a tumbledown shack) nourished young Nat's self-esteem and his longing for independence. For the slave church was not only a center for underground slave plottings against the master class, but the focal point for an entire subterranean culture the blacks sought to construct beyond the white man's control. The church was both opiate and inspiration, a place where the slaves, through their ring-shout responses and their powerful and unique spirituals, could both escape their lot and protest against it. Here they could find comfort and courage in a black man's God, an animated Spirit, a *presence* who was with them every moment of their lives. Yes, the church was a place to "get happy," one slave recalled. A place where blacks could be "free indeed, free from death, free from hell, free from work, free from white folks, free from everything."[17]

At one praise meeting, Nat was struck by a certain passage the preacher quoted from the Bible. "Seek ye the kingdom of Heaven," the preacher exclaimed, "and all things shall be added unto you." Afterward, Nat brooded over that passage. What did it mean? How did it apply to him? For weeks he prayed for light on the subject; and one day while praying at his plow Nat thought he heard a voice in the wind. It *was* a voice, he was certain of it, and as he stood rooted to the spot, he heard the Spirit call out to him as to the prophets of old, repeating the same scriptural passage the preacher had cited. Well, Nat was entranced, but he said nothing about his revelation to the other slaves, instead keeping more and more to himself and praying continuously. Then he heard it again, a wind-voice in the windswept trees: "Seek ye the kingdom of Heaven and all things shall be added unto you." At last it seemed clear to him. Because of his extraordinary qualities, Nat had been "ordained for some great purpose in the hands of the Almighty," a divine purpose that would one day be revealed to him. And he rejoiced in his communion with the Spirit and his closeness to the kingdom. And in the months and seasons that followed, he studied the Bible intensely, memorizing the books of the Old Testament, and grew to manhood with the words of the prophets roaring in his ears.[18]

Nat's mind and body traveled separate paths to man's estate. If in his daydreams the Spirit called to him from the spindrift heavens, his condition as a slave remained unchanged. Confused and resentful, he mulled over all the things said about him back on the home place ("why the boy will surely be a prophet," "look at these bumps on his head and chest," "smart as he is he'll never be of use to anybody as a slave"). And he reflected on how the Almighty had spoken to him as He had to Ezekiel in the Old Testament. Yet in spite of these miracles, here he was, twenty-one years old and still in bondage. Obviously he felt betrayed by false hopes. Obviously he thought he should be liberated like the large number of free blacks who resided in Southampton County and who were not nearly so gifted as he. Obviously he felt humiliated that he remained a lowly field hand—"a cotton patch nigger"—while less intelligent Negroes became privileged domestics, entitled to better food and living conditions and more opportunities to learn than field hands could ever have. Clearly Samuel Turner was to blame for Nat's plight—had not Master Samuel sent him to the fields and kept him there? Moreover, Turner had increased his land holdings and had bought a few additional slaves—enough to rank him as a planter—so that by 1821 it was woefully evident that he had no intention of emancipating his brilliant young Negro.

Still enslaved as a man, Nat zealously cultivated his image as a prophet, aloof, austere, and mystical. As he said later in an oral autobiographical sketch: "Having soon discovered to be great, I must appear so, and therefore studiously avoided mixing in society, and wrapped myself in mystery, devoting myself to fasting and prayer." Physically, the young mystic was a small man with what whites described as "distinct African features." Though his shoulders were broad from work in the fields, he was short, slender, and a little knock-kneed, with thin hair, a complexion like black pearl, and cavernous, shining eyes. When immersed in meditation and prayer, he seemed uninhabited, an inert statue in the corner of some slave cabin. But when he emerged from his introspections, he was alert and restless and walked with a brisk, springing step.

Inevitably, Nat began exhorting Turner's slaves in the cabins and out in the fields. The man was spellbinding. He cried out what the slaves felt inside. He now told them about his communion with the Spirit, a miracle that awed them and enhanced his reputation as a young holy man. "And they believed," Nat recalled, "and said my wisdom came from God." And as Sam and Pete, Andrew, Ephraim, and Drew gathered around, Nat announced that something large was about to happen, something that would allow him to fulfill "the great promise made to me."[19]

In 1819 a severe depression rocked the United States, and agricultural prices began an appalling downward spiral that was to last four years. The price of cotton, for example, fell from 30 cents a pound in the boom years to less than 10 cents a pound in 1823.

Virginia was especially hard hit, so that farmers and planters alike were obliged to retrench and sell their excess slaves off to the Deep South. The Panic hurt Samuel Turner, too, but he balked at selling his Negroes. Instead he hired an overseer to get more work out of them and to manage the estate more efficiently.

Evidently the overseer arrived late in 1821. It seems clear that he flogged Nat, for shortly after he came the young exhorter ran away from him. Yes, he became a fugitive, driven into Southampton's swamps by some unrecorded cruelty and private anguish. ("O, why was I born a man, of whom to make a brute!" Frederick Douglass cried when he too decided to run. "I am left in the hottest hell of unending slavery. O, God, save me! God deliver me! Let me be free! Is there any God? Why am I a slave? I will run away. I will not stand it. Get caught, or get clear, I'll try it. I have only one life to lose. I had as well be killed running as die standing.")

So Nat was gone, a slave patrol undoubtedly on his trail somewhere. And the Negroes back on Turner's farm prayed for him, recalling how Nat's father had escaped to freedom. Maybe Nat would make it too.

But thirty days later Nat returned—walked right up to the Turner house, not in the custody of the slave patrol and a pack of hounds, but of his own free will. The other slaves were astonished. No fugitive ever came back on his own. "And the negroes found fault, and murmured against me," Nat confessed later, "saying that if they had my sense they would not serve any master in the world." Nat's reply? "The Spirit appeared to me and said I had my wishes directed to the things of this world, and not to the kingdom of heaven, and that I should return to the service of my earthly master." Nat said the same to Master Samuel, who was glad to have his property back, even if he must be punished. Then with exquisite irony Nat quoted the very Biblical passage white masters liked to foist on slaves: "For he who knoweth his Master's will, and doeth it not, shall be beaten with many stripes, and thus have I chastened you."

In his oral autobiographical sketch, this was all Nat said about his runaway attempt. Yet if the other slaves grumbled about his coming back to bondage, they still regarded him with wonder and respect. In truth, the entire affair made Nat seem all the more secretive and remote. And who knows? Maybe that was what the young mystic desired all along.[20]

There may have been another reason why Nat returned to the Turner farm. At about this time he became involved with a young slave girl who resided there. Evidently her name was Cherry. We know nothing about their courtship, nothing about what picnics or praise meetings they might have attended together, nothing about their lovemaking. All that is known is that sometime after Nat's runaway incident, he and Cherry jumped over the broomstick together and so were married.[21]

In 1822 catastrophe visited the Turner place. Master Samuel, then only thirty-two years old, died of some unnamed affliction. While Nat had never respected him as he had the elder Turner, Samuel had not been a cruel master. And now he was gone, and the future was ominous for all his survivors—white and slave alike. All the Turner children were minors, so there was nobody to manage the estate. The overseer was gone now, the homestead immobilized. The slaves did not know what would happen, with farm prices still low and young Mistress Elizabeth all alone now. Then came a shocking announcement: only three domestics (one of them apparently was Nat's mother) were to remain with Elizabeth. The other twenty slaves—including Nat and Cherry—were to be sold. *Sold.* For Virginia slaves it was a terrible word: in all probability it meant that Nat and his fellow slaves would be auctioned off to some white-hatted slave trader, who would fasten them to a slave coffle and drive them chained and manacled to the brutal cotton plantations in Georgia and Alabama, there to become statistics in some planter's ledger book. Yes, they had heard about those places: for years the slave grapevine had buzzed with stories about them—grim, thousand-acre plantations, tilled by hundreds of whip-driven Negroes (the overseers are cruel down there), "Working all day, and part of the night, and up before the morning light." On some of those plantations, stories said, "niggers" were herded into sheds without regard for families and were branded like cattle.

For Virginia slaves, accustomed to a modicum of family life, Georgia seemed a living hell. "We are stolen, and sold in Georgia," a slave spiritual went. "See wives and husbands sold apart, Their children's screams will break my heart;—There's a better day a coming, Will you go along with me?"

Before going on the auction blocks, Nat and the other Turner slaves had to be valued along with the rest of Samuel's property. On the prescribed day, Nat and Cherry, Sam, Cary, Pete, Drew, Andrew, Violet, Jenny, Amy, and all the children stood in line with the livestock: 17 cows, 11 sheep, and 150 hogs. Then white men with pens and ledger books moved down the line, examining slave and animal alike and assigning each a value. ("At this moment," Frederick Douglass recalled, "I saw more clearly than ever the brutalizing effects of slavery upon both slave and slaveholder.") The whites valued Nat at $400—the price of a prime field hand. But they were unimpressed with Cherry, who was young and probably inexperienced, and set her worth at $40.

As it turned out, Nat and Cherry did not go off to Georgia on a slave gang, but remained in Southampton County within a few miles of the Turner place. Elizabeth sold Nat to one Thomas Moore and Cherry to a young fellow named Giles Reese, who rented a ramshackle farm across the woods and swamps from Moore's homestead.

For Nat and Cherry, remaining in Southampton was a mixed blessing. True, they escaped the crippling plantations in the Deep South. And true, they were not far apart and still saw one another from time to time. Nevertheless, their separation was a painful example of the wretched privations slavery placed on black people, even here in mellowed Southampton County. In time, Cherry bore children by Nat—a daughter and one or two sons. Yet Nat was doomed to live apart from them, an absentee husband and father blocked from sharing in the tough give-and-take of their everyday lives, blocked from what little they might have enjoyed together at night after work was done. At Moore's, Nat must sleep alone.[22]

Nat's new owner was a native of Southampton County, an industrious individual who aspired to become a big man in his neighborhood, to expand his holdings and acquire additional slaves. Three years before, in 1819, Moore had married Sally Francis—an excellent choice for a man on the climb, for Sally came from one of the more prominent families in the county. Her parents had amassed a thousand-acre plantation not far from Benjamin Turner's old place and had sired a brood of ten children. Nat, on his part, had known Sally since his boyhood, for he used to play with her younger brother Nathaniel, who came over to join Nat and John Clark Turner in their forest romps and expeditions. In 1815 old man Francis had died and young Nathaniel had inherited the home estate, since all the other sons except Salathial had moved on to more attractive parts. Salathial, a bachelor, got a section of the family land not far from the home place.

After Sally and Thomas Moore were married, Moore used the family connection to buy some 720 acres from the Francis estate and to secure a couple of the family field hands—Inarchy and Moses. Of course, Moore needed more slaves than that to work all his land, so when he heard about the auction over at the Turner place, he went shopping for a prime field hand—and came back with Nat. No doubt this pleased Sally. A pleasant woman, she was about Nat's age and had considerable affection for him. After all, he was a bright "boy," sober, extremely religious, and well known around the neighborhood.

Nat's new master was not a harsh man, but he clearly expected Nat to do heavy work or he would never have shelled out $400 for him. In fact, as an "expectant planter," a farmer on the rise, Moore worked his three field hands as hard as he drove himself, in a grinding effort to raise profitable crops. By 1824, Moore's labors seemed worth the effort: farm prices stabilized in Virginia and even began to rise, and the long, racking depression seemed at an end.[23]

And so Nat's days degenerated into endless, backbreaking drudgery. A sort of "all-purpose chattel," as one writer has described him, Nat built the morning fires, hauled water, fed the cows, slopped the hogs, chopped wood, raised fences, repaired fences, cleared new fields, spread manure, and grew and gathered hay for the stock. In the spring, he struggled through the damp fields behind a mule-drawn plow. Most of the summer he chopped and cut and hoed in the corn and cotton patches, battling weeds, weevils, and the weather itself. Then he had to harvest the crops before winter set in, wrestling with gunnysacks of cotton, corn, and apples which Moore loaded in his wagon and took off to sell in Jerusalem on market Saturdays.

The work never seemed to let up; it was worse than anything Nat had known back on Samuel Turner's farm. And if Nat had felt betrayed there by false hopes, he must now have been beside himself with anguish. For even after his enigmatic runaway attempt, Nat had evidently retained some vague hope that one day he might be freed. Yes, freedom. Nat understood the meaning of that word only too well. Given his prodigious knowledge of the Bible and his intelligence ("He had a mind capable of attaining anything," a white man said), it was as inevitable as time itself that Nat should crave his freedom, dream of it, fantasize about it, even when it seemed increasingly dim and distant. As another slave, Lunsford Lane, recalled: "I saw no prospect that my condition would ever be changed. Yet I used to plan in my mind from day to day, and from night to night, how I might be free." Had Nat never been born on Benjamin Turner's place, had he never learned to read the Bible and other books, had he been whipped and beaten into mindless oblivion, then maybe he would not have despised his condition so. For it was as the Preacher said in the Scriptures, "Knowledge increaseth sorrow." And here at Moore's farm Nat's sorrow was mounting daily: he was twenty-three years old, separated from his wife, caught in a maelstrom of mundane chores, the property of an ambitious young white man who was not about to unleash a $400 investment, so that freedom—so close in Nat's mind—was in reality more remote than ever.

Was *this* to be his destiny then? To spend the rest of his years behind a shitting mule in Moore's cotton patches? This could not be his purpose. There was more to his life than this. God did not intend a man of *his* gifts, *his* intelligence, *his* powers, to waste his years hoeing weeds and slopping hogs. To see his wife—poor enslaved sparrow—ordered and shoved around over at Reese's place, a victim of white people's every caprice, every whim. To toil and die like livestock (however affectionately treated) in this hypocritical Christian neighborhood, where white people gloried in the teachings of Jesus and yet discriminated against the "free coloreds" and kept all the other blacks in chains. Where slavemasters bragged about their benevolence ("In Virginia we take care of our 'niggers' ") and yet broke up families, sold Negroes off to whip-happy slave traders when money was scarce, and denied proud, godly men like Nat Turner something even the most debauched and useless poor whites enjoyed: their freedom.[24]

Part Two

GO SOUND THE JUBILEE

It was the summer or fall of 1825. For months now, Nat had seemed lost in himself, more withdrawn and concealed in mystery than ever. He avoided Moses and Inarchy, kept away from praise meetings, and passed his Sundays in his cabin or off in the woods somewhere, transported in prayer, engrossed in his Bible. He fasted ritualistically, sometimes going for days without food. Then suddenly, like the breaking of a spell, Nat emerged from his solitude and began telling the neighborhood slaves incredible things: he claimed that the Holy Spirit had again spoken to him and had opened the heavens themselves—as God had done with Ezekiel in the days of the Old Testament—and had shown Nat visions in the sky, visions so profound that they took a slave's breath away. And in the cabins at night, the slaves gathered around the young mystic, a sea of black faces looking on in awe, as Nat described what all he had felt and seen:

It began, Nat said, in the spring of that year, when he was locked in despair, working his hands to the bones in Moore's fields. At night, he read his Bible zealously, searching its pages for some answer to the riddle of his enslavement—and theirs. And for every Biblical lesson white preachers found to vindicate Negro slavery, the Scriptures contained an opposite injunction against human bondage.

There was Exodus 21:16, "And he that stealeth a man, and selleth him, or if he be found in his hand, he shall surely be put to death." There was Deuteronomy 24:7, "If a man be found stealing any of his brethren of the children of Israel, and maketh merchandise of him, or selleth him; then that thief shall die; and thou shalt put evil away from among you." And there was always the supreme example of Moses, who broke the chains of the Israelites and led them out of Egypt to the promised land. Yet in spite of these Biblical lessons slavery flourished and grew in America, washing westward across Dixie's frontiers in giant human waves. Increasingly embittered about his condition and that of his people, his imagination fired to incandescence by prolonged fasting and tales from the Old Testament, Nat began having bloody, apocalyptic visions in the woods and fields southwest of Jerusalem. "I saw white spirits and black spirits engaged in battle," Nat cried out, "and the sun was darkened—the thunder rolled in the Heavens, and blood flowed in streams—and I heard a voice saying, 'Such is your luck, such you are called to see, and let it come rough or smooth, you must surely bare it.' " Well, he was awestruck, but what did the voice mean? What must he bare? He prayed constantly for a revelation; and one day while he was plowing, the Spirit called out, "Behold me as I stand in the Heavens." And Nat looked up and saw forms of men there in a variety of attitudes, "And there were lights in the sky to which the children of darkness gave other names than what they really were—for they were the lights of the Saviour's hands, stretched forth from east to west, even as they were extended on the cross on Calvary for the redemption of sinners."[1]

Certain that Judgment Day was fast approaching, Nat strove to attain "true holiness" and "the true knowledge of faith." And once he had these, once he had been "made perfect," then the Holy Ghost was clearly in him and he felt called to preach in the slave church, to spread the true gospel among his people. And thus ordained, Nat styled himself a Baptist preacher (and so the slaves in the area accepted him) and he began conducting his own praise meetings behind Turner's Meeting House or down at Barnes's Church near the North Carolina line, singing out to his black congregation like those ringing exhorters who had inspired him in his youth.

From his slave pulpit, Nat recounted his visions in dramatic detail, telling his congregations about the warring angels in the sky, about the Savior's arms stretched across Southampton's horizon. Meanwhile he continued to fast and pray; and the Spirit responded by showing him other miracles, which he likewise reported to his congregations. While working in the field, he said, he discovered drops of blood on the corn. In the woods he found leaves with hiero-glyphic characters and numbers etched on them; other leaves con-tained forms of men—some drawn in blood—like the figures in the sky. Then once again the Holy Ghost revealed itself and Nat at last understood the meaning of these miracles. "For as the blood of Christ had been shed on this earth, and had ascended to heaven for the salvation of sinners, and was now returning to earth again in the form of dew—and as the leaves on the trees bore the impres-sion of the figures I had seen in the heavens, it was plain to me that the Saviour was about to lay down the yoke he had borne for the sins of men, and the great day of judgment was at hand."

Well, the slaves were astounded. Many of them had known Nat all his life and had always expected him to become a prophet like this. The Negroes flocked to praise meetings to hear about his mir-acles, carrying his rhapsodic voice along on a chorus of amens and hallelujahs. He earned a reputation as "a great enthusiast," whose electrifying sermons made him the most prominent slave preacher in his neighborhood.

Nat also told many white people about his visions and revelations. Some laughed them off. After all, for years a lot of white evangelists had seen similar visions and had prophesied the approach of Judg-ment Day. Other whites observed that Nat was not a certified preacher, that he was never ordained and never a member of any organized church—which was true. Nat was a self-styled black preacher—a lot of farms and plantations in Virginia had men like him. Never catch a white man believing the visions of a "nigger" preacher.[2]

Thomas and Sally Moore, for their part, evidently indulged Nat in his religious gabble and thought him harmless. He was well be-haved, honest, and smart, never drank liquor or stole anything from the Moores or anybody else. And he did his work—worked like a mule all week—and so long as he did what Moore expected of him then, all right, the "boy" could have his Sundays to preach. Many other masters in the area—the Porters, the Francis, Edwards, and Williams families—did not object to Nat's ministering to their slaves. After all, it might raise their morale, help discipline them.

Not all whites in the neighborhood, however, considered young Nat so innocuous. One chronicler later claimed that Salathial Francis—Sally's brother—deemed Nat "a negro of bad character" and warned her to keep him home on Sundays. A few other whites labeled Nat a witch doctor and accused him of "conjuring" the slaves, of employing tricks in order to frighten the superstitious creatures and make himself popular in the slave quarters. Blood on the corn indeed. Angels in the sky indeed. What humbuggery. One white later charged that Nat secretly arranged the leaves in the woods, painted these and the corn with pokeberry juice, and then showed the Negroes such skulduggery as proof of his divine importance. But Nat hotly denied that he had used conjury or voodoo tricks—"I held such things in contempt," he snapped—and insisted emphatically that his visions *had* happened, that the Spirit *had* shown him miracles in the skies and forests, and that he *had* been ordained for something larger than just plowing the white man's land.[3]

Well, if some whites scoffed at his revelations, his slave friends spoke of Preacher Nat with a reverence that fueled his prodigious pride and self-esteem. And he told them now, as 1826 came on, that the Spirit had also endowed him with a special knowledge of the seasons, the rotation of the planets, and the operation of the tides. This gave him an even greater eminence among the county's slaves, many of whom thought he could control the weather, protect them from their masters, and heal their afflictions. On one occasion, Nat himself claimed that he cured an ailing slave. How? By praying and by the imposition of his hands, Nat said.

So 1826 found Nat slaving through the week and then exhorting on Sundays. His status as a slave preacher gave him considerable freedom of movement, so that on the Sabbath he traveled around the county to meet with his flocks. And everywhere he went the signs were propitious, Judgment Day was surely close at hand. A terrible drought had set in like those recounted in the Scriptures, and the blazing skies had destroyed the white man's crops and baked his fields. The woods became dangerously combustible, and forest fires often raged out of control, filling the countryside with the smell of ash and smoke.

As Nat traveled on Sundays, he listened to the grievances and discontents of his people; he assured them that God was present in their lives, that the Spirit was here, right here in Southampton County, and that He cared for them and would not forget what He saw. One Sunday Nat would be in Jerusalem. On the following Sabbath he would be down in Cross Keys or over at Bethlehem Crossroads. When Giles Reese permitted it, Nat visited his wife and children, trying to make up in their moments together all the weeks and months they were apart. In time, Nat came to know most of the farms, plantations, swamps, ponds, paths, and roads in the county. He knew the white community, too, knew who was decent to slaves and who was cruel. He did not forget the cruel ones. Around whites he cultivated a diffident veneer, playing the roles (now serious and pious, now all Yessuh and Nossuh, all sugar and agreeableness) which whites expected of slaves. So long as Nat appeared the gifted fool, the harmless "dreamer of dreams," as one white man called him, then the white community would leave him alone to preach.

As Nat preached, he befriended several free blacks who resided on white farms as tenants or hired hands, or who scratched out a marginal existence on some little plot in the swamps and backwoods. From them he learned how limited freedom could be even for emancipated blacks, who, deprived of political and social rights, languished in a twilight zone between bondage and liberty. By 1826 or 1827, he had singled out among the slaves and free blacks some twenty men he could trust the most. These made up his innermost circle of followers, who met with him after praise meetings. He told them, "I am commissioned by Jesus Christ and act under his direction." He began preparing them for a "mission"—something large but as yet unspecified.[4]

Sometime in 1827 Nat encountered a troubled and demoralized white man named Etheldred T. Brantley. Apparently he was an

overseer on a plantation bordering Samuel Turner's farm, now operated by widow Elizabeth. Brantley was guilty of some unmentionable
"wickedness"—the records do not reveal what, but it must have been
something absolutely forbidden in white society because Brantley
could find help and salvation only in Nat's hands. Out of kindness,
the young Negro ministered to Brantley, telling him that God had
shown Nat miracles, blessed him with extraordinary powers, and
given him signs that Judgment Day was coming. All this had such
an impact on Brantley, Nat claimed, that he ceased his wickedness
altogether, whereupon sores broke out on his face, festered, and
bled. Nat then helped purge Brantley's demons, praying and fasting
with him for nine days, after which he was healed. At that, Nat
offered to baptize both Brantley and himself, declaring that the
Spirit had again appeared and said to Nat, "as the Saviour had
been baptized, so should we be also."

When the word was out, it created a sensation in the neighborhood. A white man baptized by a Negro! Well, it was unheard of,
even in tidewater Virginia, and white Christians absolutely refused
to let Nat perform the ceremony at their altars. Even the Methodists
were incensed. Even they slammed their church doors with a resounding no. But Nat was undaunted. Let the whites bar him and
Brantley from their tabernacles. He announced that he would effect
the ceremony at Pearson's Mill Pond, deep in the forests northwest
of Flat Swamp. And he promised that another miracle would occur,
that while he and Brantley were in the water, a dove would descend
from heaven and light on his head.

On the prescribed day, Nat took Brantley to Pearson's Pond,
where an interracial crowd had gathered—the slaves to see their
holy man save a white sinner, the whites to mock and curse them.
As Nat put it later: "We went down to the water together, in the
sight of many who reviled us, and were baptised by the Spirit." No
dove descended from the heavens as Nat had vowed, but no matter:
the slaves had seen him do a spectacular thing in christening a
white man and then himself. And Nat too was pleased with his
performance. "I rejoiced greatly," he said, "and gave thanks to
God."[5]

Deep down, though, Nat smoldered with bitterness and resentment. For in spite of the Brantley episode, in spite of all his visions and all his revelations, he was still Moore's property. He was still a cotton-patch nigger. He was still slaving behind a mule. Whites did not know it, but behind Nat's well-mannered façade was a messianic individual who felt himself driven into some corner of slavery from which there was no return. He was like a powerful angel whose wings were nailed to the floor. Only in his imagination was he free —free to live in the pages of the Old Testament, to identify with Biblical prophets, to envision himself a singular man of destiny in the other world of his mind.

But in the real world he was a gifted and furious unknown— blocked from his potential by an impregnable wall, a man whose only claim to immortality was his eminence among some slaves in an isolated Virginia backwater. Whose only act of defiance was to baptize a desperate white man in the face of a crowd.

Yes, rage burned in him—fed by the prodigious chasm between what he was and what he aspired to be in this, the only life he had. And out of his frustrations, out of his fastings and Bible fantasies, there came on May 12, 1828, the most epochal vision of all. Suddenly "I heard a loud noise in the heavens," Nat recalled, "and the Spirit instantly appeared to me and said the Serpent was loosened, and Christ had laid down the yoke he had borne for the sins of men, and that I should take it on and fight against the Serpent, for the time was fast approaching when the first should be last and the last should be first." Now at last it was clear. By signs in the heavens would Jehovah show Nat when to commence his great work, whereupon "I should arise and prepare myself, and slay my enemies with their own weapons." And once he had accomplished this divine task, once he had crushed his white enemies and defeated the Serpent (which symbolized Satan himself), then Nat Turner would bring on the years of Jubilee when those who had been first—the white masters—would become subservient to the blacks who had been last. *Thus was Nat's mission in this world finally revealed to him.* But until God gave him a sign to begin, Nat should keep his lips sealed, even among his wife and closest followers.

But his work was too momentous for him to remain entirely silent. One day he announced to Thomas Moore that the slaves ought to be free and would be "one day or other." Shocked at such rebellious talk from a slave, Moore took Nat to the shed and gave him a thrashing.[6]

For a slave to talk about Negro liberation, within earshot of other slaves, was indeed a grave offense in these dark and uncertain years. To Southern whites, many of them, the 1820s were not only a time of depression and drought, but a time when slave rebelliousness again seemed on the rise. Like those anxious years surrounding Santo Domingo and the Gabriel conspiracy in Richmond, insurrection scares periodically rocked Virginia and the Carolinas, especially the South Carolina low country, where slaves heavily outnumbered whites. In 1822 Charleston authorities uncovered the most dangerous insurrection plot since Gabriel's, one that sent shock waves through the rice and luxury cotton plantations along the Atlantic coast. The leader of the conspiracy was Denmark Vesey, a hulking, literate carpenter who had bought his freedom, traveled a good deal, and read profusely. Among the things he read were the momentous congressional debates that resulted in the 1820 Missouri Compromise, debates that turned not just on the status of slavery in the Missouri country, but on the very nature of the institution itself. If many Southerners were appalled at such open discussion of slavery, Vesey himself was inspired. He talked about the Missouri debates with his black friends in Charleston's slums. An aging mulatto with several wives and many children still in bondage, Vesey raged about their condition and lashed out against the institution of slavery. He lectured fellow blacks on the Declaration of Independence, asserted that slavery "is against the Bible," and rebuked Negroes for taking white insults, for stepping into muddy streets so that whites could pass on the sidewalks. When some blacks sputtered that they were slaves, Vesey snapped back, "You deserve to remain slaves."

Soon he gathered around him a number of trusted followers, most of them house servants and black mechanics who belonged to Charleston's African Church. Here they plotted a revolt that would involve Negroes in the city as well as hundreds of slaves on the outlying plantations. One of Vesey's chief lieutenants was an Angolese witch doctor named Gullah Jack. A small man with tiny limbs and prodigious whiskers, he was supposed to play an indispensable role once the revolt began, for his grotesque appearance, savage gestures, and fierce glances would intimidate slave soldiers and keep them in line. Jack gave each recruit a crab claw to carry on the day of the insurrection, contending that the claw embodied the power of his African gods and would protect the slaves from the white man's bullets.

Vesey's strategy called for a surprise attack against Charleston, to be executed by a concert of city and country slaves. At the stroke of midnight, when the sentinel called out that all was well, the insurgents would leap into action: organized into six battle units, they would capture the guardhouse and arsenal, ambush slothful patrols, seize the major roads, and ax and shoot those masters who ran out of their mansions to resist. But beyond that plans were vague: one lieutenant wanted to hold Charleston against white counterattacks, but Vesey hoped to sail away to Haiti.

Like the Gabriel conspiracy, the revolt never came off. Once again, communications broke down between the urban leaders and the rural slaves out on the big tidewater plantations. Once again, loyal house servants betrayed the conspirators and whispered into white ears what was in the air. At once five military companies invaded the slums, throwing the entire city into a panic. In their lavish town mansions, the planters went through an unforgettable night, plagued with the specter of rape and murder, of a Santo Domingo boiling up right here in Charleston. In the end, the authorities arrested most of the rebels, hanged Vesey and thirty-four alleged collaborators, and banished thirty-seven other blacks from the state. Though Charleston had narrowly escaped a Negro revolution, the gentry realized only too well that it could happen again. "Let it never be forgotten," cried one white man, "that 'our NEGROES are truly the *Jacobins* of the country; that they are the *anarchists* and the *domestic enemy;* the *common enemy of civilized society,* and the barbarians who would, IF THEY COULD, become the DESTROYERS *of our race.'* "

After that the tidewater gentry formed vigilance committees to watch the slaves, and whites throughout the low country kept their muskets loaded. The South Carolina legislature also passed a law which imprisoned black sailors who came to Charleston on British ships, because those sailors had been to Haiti and might incite a slave revolt. Then came the Charleston fire scare. On Christmas Eve, 1825, a conflagration whipped and roared on King Street, consuming $80,000 worth of property. Afterward, almost every night for six months, arsonists set fire to one Charleston building after another, reviving all the macabre memories of Denmark Vesey. Whites, of course, insisted that slave dissidents were behind the nightly terrorism and convicted at least three Negroes for it. Three years later, up the coast at Georgetown, white authorities uncovered another insurrection plot, packed the jails with Negro suspects, and hanged six and perhaps many more. Never, it seemed, had the slaves plotted and sabotaged so boldly and so often as they were doing now.

In point of fact, only a small minority of slaves were involved in organized conspiracies during the 1820s. But they attracted all the attention and helped create exaggerated fears among anxious whites, particularly along South Carolina's coastal black belt. There a planter who kept his slave quarters under constant surveillance never knew what those inscrutable blacks were plotting. Was there a Denmark Vesey among his own people? his own property? Would they attack him in the dark of some sinister night and slit his throat and rape his wife and daughters? It was menacing enough to make him want to sell out, even though his rice and luxury sea-island cotton were commanding good prices, and move out to Alabama or Mississippi, where insurrection scares were not so frequent.[7]

Many Southerners, searching about for scapegoats, blamed slave unrest on an abolitionist movement now gaining momentum in the North and upper South. Beleaguered Carolinians, for their part, charged that "oily tongued" abolitionist agents were behind South Carolina's slave conspiracies, that these agents met with blacks at night, got them drunk, and filled their spinning heads with dangerous talk about civil rights. Other Southerners feared that the antislavery movement, though incipient in the 1820s, would some day lead to an abolitionist take-over of the federal government, forced emancipation, and the wholesale destruction of the South's slave-based social order. In truth, the antislavery clamor did seem to be rising in the 1820s. Benjamin Lundy, a Baltimore Quaker, not only started his abolitionist newspaper, *The Genius of Universal Eman-*

cipation, but also established several antislavery societies here in the South. And those troublesome "free coloreds" were also speaking out. In New York, they were now publishing the first Negro newspaper ever to appear in America—an antislavery sheet called *Freedom's Journal.* Along with the Quakers and other antislavery groups, the free blacks were gathering antislavery petitions and sending them to Congress. And petitions from various colonization societies were likewise piling up there.

Southern leaders were extremely alarmed about these documents. Since the 1790s (that decade of the Santo Domingo revolt), Georgia and South Carolina congressmen had warned that antislavery petitions were "merely an entering wedge for total emancipation." After the Missouri debates and the Vesey plot, Carolina congressmen and their Southern allies, exhibiting "a morbid sensitivity" to the small and relatively harmless antislavery attack, moved to strangle all abolitionist and colonization petitions. Open discussion of slavery in Congress, they feared, would result in the triumph of abolition; it would rage across the highly susceptible free states, and even invade the South. Soon the slaves would be screaming for freedom or rising up in rebellion, and intimidated whites might indeed support emancipation to save their lives. So Southern congressmen labored assiduously to get those petitions permanently tabled and to suppress all discussion about the peculiar institution. Only through "a conspiracy of silence," it seemed, could slavery be maintained and the Southern master class protected.

There were other dangers, too. In 1828 Congress passed a new protective tariff which raised duties on imported raw materials and manufactured goods. The new tariff exasperated a lot of people in all sections of America, but those most opposed to it were embattled Southern agrarians. Ironically enough, many Southerners had once supported protection in hopes that it would stimulate industrial growth in Dixie as well. In fact, the first protective tariff—that of 1816—had largely been the work of South Carolinians like John C. Calhoun, then a staunch nationalist. But in the ensuing years, protection seemed to benefit only manufactures in the Northeast, which generally increased in wealth and population while older Southern states like South Carolina suffered economic stagnation. In time most Southerners, especially the cotton growers, came to regard the tariff as a discriminatory and unconstitutional device which taxed the South to enrich the North. Thus when an even higher tariff appeared in 1828, Southern cotton growers howled in protest and demanded that this "abomination" be rescinded. While cries against the tariff echoed across Dixie (and across the agrarian Midwest as well), the reaction was the loudest and most combustible in depression-plagued South Carolina. Here angry cotton growers blamed the tariff for all their economic woes, from relatively low staple cotton prices to soaring production costs. But the tariff was not the only grievance Carolinians nursed against the federal government—and the Northern states beyond. Equally noxious, declared one Carolina paper, were those Yankee abolitionists who interfered "with our domestic policy" and who must "be met with something more than words." South Carolina's powerful rice planters emphatically agreed and flailed the tariff with a vengeance—but not because it hurt them economically, for rice and luxury cotton continued to sell at high prices. Still rattled about the insurrection scares, low-country planters viewed the tariff as the first step toward Northern domination and federal usurpation. If the Yankees could pass higher and higher tariffs, what was to stop them from some day enacting a congressional abolition law—and justifying it by the same nationalistic arguments advanced in favor of protection? With their heavy slave concentrations, Carolina rice planters shuddered at the prospects and zealously joined with the cotton growers in demanding that federal power be decisively curbed. Even Calhoun conceded that the "real cause of the present unhappy state of things" was "the peculiar domestic institution of the Southern states." To protect his cherished South (and to ensure his political future in South Carolina), Calhoun revised his position and formulated a potent new interpretation of state rights: in the *South Carolina Exposition and Protest,* which he secretly authored in 1828, Calhoun championed the right of a "sovereign" state to nullify any federal law which imperiled its welfare or "domestic institutions"—namely, Negro slavery. A committee of the South Carolina legislature published and circulated the document as a warning to Yankees and abolitionist agitators: you pass national laws that menace us and our way of life and we will nullify them. And beyond nullification, if South Carolina's grievances were not redressed, lay the road to secession and potential civil war.[8]

While Carolina planters inveighed against the tariff, there were other portentous developments. In 1829 a convention met in Richmond, Virginia, to draft a new state constitution. There was talk along the slave grapevine that Virginia's blacks might be liberated. Their hopes were crushed, though, when the delegates refused even to consider emancipation and restricted suffrage to whites only . . . conclusive proof that Virginia, contrary to an enduring myth, was moving not toward emancipation but away from it. After the convention adjourned, Virginia crawled with rumors that the slaves were about to revolt. How many of these reports were true and how many the product of frightened white imaginations is impossible to tell. The governor, for his part, contended that "these rumors have been much talked about by the slaves themselves, and have probably increased the spirit of insubordination." Alarmed, he advised that Virginia put herself on a strong military footing. As a consequence, militia companies and volunteer organizations went on the alert in fifty-nine Virginia counties as well as in Richmond, Petersburg, Norfolk, and Lynchburg.[9]

There was also a strong backlash against "incendiary" abolitionist publications thought to be infiltrating from the North. In the Southern white's view, the most infamous of these documents was David Walker's *Appeal to the Colored Citizens of the World,* published in Boston in 1829. Walker was a free Negro who had traveled extensively, studied history books and the Bible, and lectured at Negro meetings in Boston. His pamphlet smoked and blazed with black militance, with religious and revolutionary zeal. Addressing himself to Negroes in North and South alike, Walker exclaimed: "Are we MEN!! I ask you, O my brethren! are we MEN? Did our Creator make us to be slaves to dust and ashes . . . ? Have we any other master but Jesus Christ?" He upbraided Thomas Jefferson for his racial views. He hotly denied that he wanted to fornicate with white daughters. "Before the Lord," he growled, "I would not give *a pinch of snuff* to be married to any white person I ever saw in all the days of my life." He asserted that the British were the best friends black people ever had, even though the British "sorely" oppressed them in the West Indies. All the same, the British had done a hundred times more than any other nation to ameliorate the blacks' condition. And America? That land of tyrants! That land of Christian hypocrites! "I ask O ye Christians," Walker admonished American whites, "if God gives you peace and tranquility, and suffers you thus to go on afflicting us and our children, who have never given you the least provocation,—Would he be to us *a God of Justice?* If you will allow that we are MEN, who feel for each other, does not the blood of our fathers and of us their children, cry aloud to the Lord of Sabbath against you, for the cruelties and murders with which you have, and do continue to afflict us?" And he mounted a furious verbal assault against Southern slavery itself, "the most wretched abject servile slavery, that ever a people was afflicted with since the foundation of the world," and summoned the slaves to rise up and slay "our cruel oppressors and murderers," those white masters who have "stolen our rights, and kept us ignorant of Him and His divine worship." And after a crescendo of outrage and exhortation, Walker climaxed his *Appeal* by quoting from the Declaration of Independence, that "ALL MEN ARE CREATED EQUAL, *that they are endowed by their Creator with certain unalienable rights; that among these are life, liberty, and the pursuit of happiness.*"[10]

It wasn't long, of course, before Southern whites learned about Walker's *Appeal.* Inevitably, rumors circulated in Dixie that abolitionist agents had been arrested in the act of distributing this "dangerous" pamphlet and that some slaves had been caught looking at it. In reaction to Walker's *Appeal,* Virginia and North Carolina enacted laws against teaching slaves to read and write. Passed in April, 1831, after John Floyd had become governor, the Virginia law was not yet strictly enforced. Although alarmists claimed it ought to be, for there were reports of "extraordinary slave unrest" in Wilmington, Delaware, and other places in the upper South. Newspapers blamed the Delaware troubles not only on Walker's pamphlet, but on white and black preachers who aroused the slaves with false promises, who asserted that "measures have been taken towards their emancipation on a certain and not distant day."

Nor were threats to Southern slaveowners confined to preachers, abolitionists, and insurrectionaries in the United States. In truth, the 1820s seemed a time of revolutionary upheaval all over the Western World. In England, a high-powered abolitionist movement was under way to liberate the slaves in Britain's West Indies. And revolutions had not only broken out in Poland, Turkey, Greece,

Italy, Spain, and France, but had blazed across Spain's ramshackle South American empire as well, resulting in new republics whose capitals rang with the rhetoric of freedom and independence. Moreover, some of these fledgling nations were foes of slavery: the Republic of Mexico, for example, produced laws and promulgations which abolished slavery throughout the nation—including Mexico's subprovince of Texas. While American slaveholders there managed to circumvent the laws and retain their chattel, they worried about Mexico's antislavery posturings—and so did some Southerners back home as well. For abolitionism seemed to be closing in on the South from all directions. Worse still, bona fide insurrections had broken out in several areas of Latin America where slavery remained—the inevitable results, Southerners would argue, of abolitionist and revolutionary turbulence.[11]

Well, in so menacing a world, Southern whites must find ways to cope. As always, a lot of them refused to talk about troublesome events, told themselves nothing was wrong, and went on about their business. Other whites acted as though conditions were not so bad as they appeared. Sure, there had been insurrection scares in the South, but the authorities had found out about the conspirators and hanged them before anything dreadful had happened. At least Southerners could take some solace in the fact that, in this decade of ferment all across the Western World, the South had experienced no sustained rebellion of the magnitude of Santo Domingo.

Certainly this was the attitude a lot of Virginians adopted. If insurrection panics had shaken Norfolk and Petersburg, if accounts of additional slave plots inhabited newspaper reports and letters to the editor, the Old Dominion had still escaped the large-scale conspiracies that had rocked South Carolina. In fact, in spite of all the rumors of slave disaffection and discontent, Virginians were quick to tell themselves that "their people" had never been happier. And why shouldn't they be? After all, if Virginians often fretted about Negro resistance, many of them strove to treat their own slaves with kindness and Christian duty. By Southern white standards, enlightened benevolence flourished all over the Old Dominion . . . most whites who lived there would tell you that as a fact. Virginians allowed a few slave schools to operate—even after that became a crime—and almost without complaint permitted slaves to hold illegal religious meetings. Why? Because permissiveness, many Virginians argued, was still the best way to prevent rebelliousness. If you treated your darkies well and gave them special privileges (their families, their Sundays off), they would be too full of gratitude to poison your well or stab you in the back. And once whites could believe that, they could sleep through the night.[12]

Still, Virginians were taking no chances. Even though their slaves, they contended, were too happy and too submissive to strike back, the state was a veritable military garrison. By 1831 it had a militia force of some 100,000 men to guard against insurrection. True, the militia needed renovation. And true, since many militiamen had not cared for their weapons properly, most of the muskets had been stored in centrally located armories like that in Richmond. But even so the militia remained a potent instrument of destruction—something most slaves understood only too well. In addition, the state had numerous volunteer military organizations that could mobilize at the first sign of insurrection. There were also the county patrols which chased down runaways and checked out reports of local slave disturbances. And behind these state agencies was the United States garrison at Fortress Monroe, across from Norfolk, and the potential military power of the federal government itself. To suppress insurrections, after all, was one of the main reasons why the federal government could mobilize the militia of the several states, as the Constitution expressly stated.[13]

Down in backwater Southampton County, where Nat Turner received a thrashing for mouthing the unspeakable, whites were caught in the same paradox: most adult males belonged to the militia and turned out for the annual drills, yet hardly anyone in Southampton thought a slave rebellion would happen here. Why, look at the history of the county: only that one "revolt" back in 1799 to mar an otherwise spotless record so far as insurrections went. Beyond that, only seven slaves had ever been convicted of crimes, and of these three had been executed and four transported out of the region. Most of the neighboring counties had similar records, so that Southampton whites regarded insurrection as some unimaginable calamity that happened to somebody else. *Their* blacks, they insisted, had never been more content, more docile. Yes, they did get a little too emotional and extravagant in their religious meetings these days.

And once in a while you had to whip a slave for getting out of line —as Moore did with Nat—just to keep the darkies from getting any ideas. But all a white man really had to worry about here was whether he had enough brandy on hand for the winter and whether prices for crops would remain stable through picking time.[14]

If Southampton whites carried on as usual, believing that things were quiet in their neighborhood, Preacher Nat was certain that these were exceptional times. Not only had he seen epochal visions, but he had his ear to the slave grapevine. He knew about Denmark Vesey and other slave conspirators. He knew that insurrection scares had jolted several Virginia communities. And while no evidence exists that he ever read or even heard about Walker's *Appeal,* Nat felt the same frustrations that Walker did and was swept up in similar religious and revolutionary fervor. And so Nat waited, his lips sealed, for the heavens to open up—for the Almighty to give him the sign to do exactly what Walker demanded of slaves: to stand "like MEN, *and not brutes,"* and fight for their liberation as God wanted them to do.[15]

But for some reason Jehovah showed him no further signs, and Nat was carried along in the ebb and flow of ordinary life. In 1828 Thomas Moore died and Nat and the other slaves—Moses, Inarchy, Lucy, Olive, and Sonia—all became the legal property of Moore's nine-year-old son, Putnam. Now bonded to a young boy, Nat must have been mortified.

About a year later, in October, 1829, Sally married a local wheelwright named Joseph Travis. Joseph soon moved to Sally's place, set up his carriage business, and assumed supervision of the Moore slaves, which with his own gave him command of seventeen Negroes. Although Nat and the other Moore slaves legally belonged to Putnam, Travis had full control over them until the boy became of age.

So it was that Nat, a sort of twice-owned chattel, sank deeper into slavery than ever. Yet as always he hid his resentment. He did not complain or say anything "incendiary" in the presence of whites, not any more. Instead, he played the "good nigger" and won Travis's "greatest confidence."

Joseph himself was a kind master—even Nat said so. As Moore had done, Joseph permitted Nat to retain the last name of Turner —a remarkable thing since slaves almost always adopted the surname of their current owner. But Nat had grown up in the neighborhood known as Benjamin Turner's bright and pious Nat, and the last name had stuck. No matter who owned him, he was always known as Nat Turner, the "smart nigger," whom whites generally regarded with a mixture of disdain, curiosity, indulgence, humor, and even a little respect. They let him have a last name.[16]

So that Travis could work freely on his carriages, he hired an overseer to manage the farm and drive the slaves. Contrary to popular belief, Nat did not become a skilled domestic—did not labor with Travis in the wheelwright shop—but remained in the fields as always. But so long as he did his work there and stayed out of trouble and gave no back talk, Travis let Nat continue with his preaching on the Sabbath. No doubt Sally had something to do with his decision, because she still had considerable affection for Nat no matter what he'd said about freedom in 1828. And so Nat kept on as a field-hand preacher, a cotton-patch prophet, all the while carrying in his mind the profound knowledge that soon, very soon indeed, God would give him a sign to commence his divine mission of death.

In February, 1831, there was an eclipse of the sun. Southampton County stirred with excitement, and the superstitious of both races cried out, *Was it the end of the world?* For Nat, the eclipse was the sign he had been waiting for—could there be any doubt? Removing the seal from his lips, he gathered around him four slaves in whom he had complete trust—Hark, Nelson, Henry, and Sam—and confided what he was called to do. They became his closest lieutenants, whose job was to spread discontent among the Negroes in the area, to single out the more spirited blacks and make them ripe for rebellion.[17]

All four were disaffected slaves—Nat had chosen them well—and all evidently were active in the slave church and underground. Moreover, all four were field hands like Nat. Of them only Henry was a "plantation" slave; the others resided on farms with modest numbers of adult blacks (around five or six) and thus had direct contact with their masters. Chief among the lieutenants was Hark

Travis, who lived at the Travis place with Nat and fifteen other slaves, over half of them children. Valued at a higher price than Nat himself, Hark was a proud, powerful individual, "a regular black Apollo," whites said. He had once belonged to Thomas Moore and so had been friends with Nat for some time now.

Next was Nelson Williams, the property of Jacob Williams, who owned a small farm in another neighborhood some four miles southwest of Jerusalem. Jacob possessed only six Negroes, including Nelson, yet somehow employed an overseer named Caswell Worrell who lived with his family in a forest cabin near Jacob's homestead. Though whites claimed that Nelson enjoyed special privileges, that he could come and go with considerable ease for a slave, he smoldered with resentment toward Williams and Worrell, who worked with him in the fields. A leader among the slaves in his section, Nelson was a sorcerer who claimed the power to foretell future events . . . like storms and droughts. Like wars and insurrections.

Not much is known about the other lieutenants—Sam Francis and Henry Porter. Sam belonged to young Nathaniel Francis, who operated the family homestead and held some fifteen slaves. Sam and Nat Turner had frequent contact since their masters had family ties—Sally Travis was young Francis's sister, a relation that permitted the family slaves considerable freedom of movement between the farms. Henry Porter likewise resided nearby, and Nat apparently chose him and Sam less for their leadership qualities than for their proximity and reliance—both would follow him anyplace, do what he asked. Moreover, Henry's master—Richard Porter—was a planter who boasted of thirty slaves, ten of them men. Henry was to approach the more unhappy males and inform them that Preacher Nat was going to do something large very soon.

Evidently Nat also revealed something about his mission to several free Negroes who lived near him—among them Billy Artis and Barry Newsom. And Nat discussed his work with Cherry, too, telling her that he had been plotting insurrection in his mind since 1828 and that God had now given him a sign to begin.

Meantime Nat met with his Chosen Four after Negro religious meetings and rehearsed with them how the time had finally arrived when the first should be last and the last should be first . . . how God had selected them, through the Prophet Nat, to fight the satanic

Serpent and overthrow the white people and inaugurate the years of Jubilee. To bolster discipline and morale, Nat assumed the title of "General Nat," and Nelson likewise became known as "General Nelson" and Hark as "General Moore." Together they pored over a crude map of Southampton County which Nat had drawn with berry juice. They examined Nat's religious papers—remarkable papers, papers containing numerological calculations and drawings of the crucifix and the sun. And they compiled a list of eighteen or nineteen Negroes who could be counted on when operations began.

Out of their deliberations emerged a target date: they would commence the work of death on July 4, whose connotation Nat clearly understood. (Surprisingly enough, rumors now circulated among the county slaves that another war with England was about to break out and that a British invasion would result in their liberation.) But Nat and his lieutenants could not agree on details. They formed and rejected so many plans that Nat's mind was affected. He was seized with dread. He fell sick, and Independence Day came and passed.

Later Nat said he dreaded to begin so gruesome a mission. For who knew what the outcome would be for certain? Who knew how many whites—and how many blacks—would die once the conflagration was roaring? And these were not strangers—these whites who must perish in Nat's holy war. Many of them he had known and lived with all his life. Even if they owned him like a mule, even if as in the story of Ezekiel the people of Jerusalem had fallen into abominable sins and must be punished by a divine and terrible vengeance, he did not think he could do it. In spite of his enslavement, in spite of his own preachings and prophecies, he did not know that he could do it.[18]

On Saturday, August 13, 1831, there was another sign. Because of some atmospheric disturbance, the sun grew so dim it could be looked at directly. Then with the air "a dead calm" the sun seemed to change colors—now pale green, now blue, now white—and there was much excitement and consternation in the eastern United States from South Carolina to New York. In Philadelphia, fearful whites proclaimed it "a sad augury of coming evil." In Richmond, newspapers contended that the sun's sinister appearance could be explained scientifically. But others there, adhering to predictions of the ancient astrologers, thought a bloody war was at hand and prophesied the end of the world.

By Saturday afternoon, the sun was like an immense ball of polished silver, and the air was moist and hazy. Then a black spot could be seen, apparently on the sun's surface—a phenomenon that greatly aroused the slaves in southeastern Virginia. For Nat Turner, watching transfixed on the Travis farm, the spot was like a black hand across the sun. Yes, it was Jehovah again, commanding him by "signed omens" to rise against his white enemies. Yes, God wanted him to move. No matter how calamitous the work might become, God wanted him to move. With awakened resolution, he told his lieutenants that "as the black spot passed over the sun, so shall the blacks pass over the earth."[19]

Although Nat tried to keep details of his plot a secret (not even the Chosen Four knew yet of a specific plan), the word was out in the slave quarters that something was about to happen—something connected with the day of the black sun. And through the following week there were telling scenes like these:

Scene one: It is Sunday morning, August 14. A black preacher is exhorting a slave congregation at Barnes's Church near the North Carolina line. Whites who pass the church observe that the blacks are "disorderly." They have taken offense at something, though whites do not know what. Later some whites thought Nat Turner was the preacher.

Scene two: It is Monday, on Solomon Parker's farm. A female slave overhears several men talking in guarded tones in one of the Negro cabins. They agree that "if the black people come this way we will join and help kill the white people." The girl has heard such rebellious talk before: after a religious meeting back in May, several slaves gathered around a well and two snarled, "God damn the white people they have reigned long enough." Unobtrusively, the girl enters the cabin, notes that two of the slaves come from neighboring Sussex County. As the slaves talk, one says that his master recently cropped his ears and will be cropped in return before the year is out. The men turn, notice the girl. They warn her that what she's heard is a secret. If she tells the whites, they will think her a conspirator, too, and will shoot her.

Scene three: It is Thursday, August 18. Nelson Williams, the sorcerer and one of Nat's chief lieutenants, walks up to his overseer and brazenly announces that white people should "look out and take care of themselves—that something would happen before long." Then he goes off, apparently immune to the white man's wrath.

Scene four: It is Saturday night, August 20. One of Ben Edwards's slaves—a man named Isham—takes another slave aside and whispers, "General Nat is going to rise and murder all the whites." They must join him, Isham says. Otherwise the white people will kill them both.[20]

It is impossible to say how many such scenes transpired in that fateful week. A majority of Southampton's slaves probably knew little or nothing about Nat's designs. But available records do suggest that several Negroes both in Southampton and in adjoining counties in Virginia and North Carolina received word that something apocalyptic was in the wind, but did not know when or how Nat intended to move. No doubt they reacted like the slaves on Parker's farm: if Nat came their way, they would rise with him and fight against the whites. If not, they would continue day-to-day resistance, sabotaging plows, faking sickness, and acting lazy.[21]

Meanwhile, in other parts of Virginia, slaves who knew nothing about Nat Turner, nothing at all, protested their condition in the usual ways. At praise meetings throughout the whole summer of that year, black preachers sounded the trumpets of despair and discontent. And in Prince William, Stafford, and King George counties along the Potomac River, in the sweltering stone quarries there, the slaves sang a spiritual called "The African Hymn," composed by the Reverend Shadrack Bassett. The lyrics were more prophetic than the slaves in northern Virginia could have known:

> *We shall not always weep and groan*
> *And wear these slavish chains of woe,*
> *There's a better day that's coming*
> *Come and go along with me.*

> *Good Lord, O when shall slavery cease*
> *And these poor souls enjoy their peace,*
> *Good Lord, break the power.*
> *Come and go along with me.*

O! come, ye Africans, be wise
We'll join the armies in the skies!
We'll ruin Satan's kingdom
    Come and go along with me.

King Jesus now comes riding in,
He bids his army sound again.
They will ruin Satan's kingdom
    Come and go along with me.

I will pursue my journey's end,
For Jesus Christ is still my friend,
O, may this friend go with me.
    Come and go along with me—
    Go sound the Jubilee.[22]

Part Three

JUDGMENT DAY

Sunday, August 21, dawned warm and clear in Richmond, with a scent of burning wood in the wind. Richmond's dirt streets, rutted and dung-ridden, were crowded this morning as white and slave families gathered in the capital to visit, hear preaching, and picnic on the grassy common. Of course the shops and markets—and the slave auction blocks—were closed this morning in observance of the Sabbath.

Over in the Executive Mansion, situated near the armory and Capitol building, Governor John Floyd made a brief diary entry about the weather and prepared to spend a quiet, leisurely Sunday. Now forty-eight years old, Floyd was a physician in politics, a refined, cranky individual, of somewhat delicate health, who carried a singular dislike for illiterate politicians—especially if they were United States Senators. "I say a Senator ought to be a man of education who could speak and write his own language at least grammatically," the governor contended. "What resistance could fifty illiterate men make against one learned and talented man, unless indeed it comes to brute force, and then, in that case, man is leveled with the brutes, in which contest, a jack ass would be greater than half a dozen men." A contemporary portrait shows Floyd as a slender man of sartorial elegance, with a receding hairline, sloping nose, thick eyebrows, and an expression of cultivated displeasure. A native of Jefferson County with Old Dominion ancestry, he had attended Pennsylvania's Dickinson College and had gone on to study medicine at the University of Pennsylvania, where he had graduated. He had served in the War of 1812 as a military surgeon, practiced medicine in southwest Virginia, represented his state in the lower house of Congress, and had supported Andrew Jackson in the bitter Presidential election of 1828, only to break with the old patriot over the tariff and other federal issues. After gaining the Virginia governorship early in 1830, Floyd had worked hard to build up the state's economy. In spite of the tariff of abominations and the economic vicissitudes of the last decade, Virginia now enjoyed some degree of stability. In fact, farm prices had actually risen a little in 1831, and Floyd fervently hoped that Virginians would soon be tilling the bounteous fields of prosperity. Yes, under Floyd's leadership Virginia's economy seemed on the upswing. And why should it not be? Was he not an unflagging champion of commercial growth and expansion? Did he not advocate river and harbor improvements? Call for the construction of more canals, turnpikes, and newfangled railroads, in order to unify the state and increase exports, in order to connect town with countryside, tidewater with piedmont, coastal ports with those fertile mountain farms beyond the Blue Ridge? When the legislature met in December, Floyd would offer a bold economic program—a network of internal improvements, subsidized by the state—that would make Virginia a booming commercial empire.

Virginia's future, though, depended a great deal on national politics and the next President (1832 was a Presidential election year). Frankly, the governor favored rhetorical and icy-eyed John C. Calhoun of South Carolina, currently Jackson's Vice-President and the chief spokesman for state rights and nullification, particularly in his fight against the 1828 tariff—and the abolitionist menace a lot of South Carolina nullifiers saw beyond it. Floyd, too, was a proponent of state sovereignty and nullification, arguing that the states should "interpose" their authority to arrest unconstitutional measures and restrain federal power. So there was no doubt in Floyd's mind that Calhoun would make a better chief executive than the feisty, unlettered Tennessean who now disgraced the White

House. At night, in the quiet of his candle-lit study, Floyd confided to his diary what he thought of Andrew Jackson. Once the governor considered him capable of greatness—of becoming another Thomas Jefferson—but now Floyd felt nothing but resentment and pity for him. For Jackson had proved himself an obnoxious dimwit who ignored the "brilliant" counsel of Calhoun and his Southern colleagues in the Administration and who had surrounded himself with "wretches of narrow minds" like John Eaton and Martin Van Buren, the latter a conniving Yankee. Ever since the beginning of Jackson's Presidency, Calhoun and "little Van" had engaged in a rancorous power struggle for Jackson's ear and the Presidential succession. But alas, the President had rejected Floyd's hero. He had accused Calhoun of being personally disloyal to him. He had blamed the Vice-President for the scandalous quarrels over Peggy Eaton. And he had renounced Calhoun's cherished nullification arguments, devised by the Vice-President to protect the South from Yankee abolitionist and economic aggrandizement. Though himself a Southern slaveowner with a strong respect for the rights of the states, Old Hickory refused to traffic with nullifiers or potential disunionists. "Our Federal Union—it must be preserved!" he warned Calhoun at a Jefferson birthday dinner in 1830. The following year—in the summer of 1831, in fact—Jackson had reorganized his Cabinet, forcing Calhoun's adherents out of the Administration and leaving the harried Vice-President to wither on the vine. While the President intended to run for re-election in 1832, Van Buren, that "sly fox," was plainly Jackson's heir apparent for 1836.

All of which upset Governor Floyd. In his view, the President was a mule-headed tyrant who, in disregarding Calhoun's sacrosanct doctrines of state rights and nullification, had "cut up" the Constitution itself and imperiled the balance and harmony that existed between the national government and the sovereign states. In Floyd's opinion, the federal government under "King Andrew" had usurped power left and right, thus allowing the majority to run roughshod over the minority. First and foremost, Jackson had permitted the damnable tariff to continue in operation. That most "unjust and unequal" enactment discriminated against exporting states like Virginia and so took from Floyd's constituents "profits they have earned by their own industry." And that was unconstitutional if anything was. Moreover, the Jackson Administration wanted to distribute surplus federal funds among the states. Such a plan, Floyd contended, would again penalize exporting states like the Old Dominion, which contributed much to the federal treasury, and would work to the unfair advantage of nonexporting states which brought in very little federal revenue. Now *that,* Floyd believed, was usurpation. And unless something were done about it, such federal aggrandizement would go on and on until it wrecked America's sacred political system—that loose confederation of sovereign states which Floyd thought the Founding Fathers had established. And the only way to preserve the system, of course, was for the American people to embrace Calhoun's principles, to use their states as constitutional watchdogs against the monster government in Washington.

What bothered Floyd the most was what federal "usurpation" might do to Virginia's economic growth. Unlike a number of South Carolina nullifiers, who had a pathological fear of abolitionists and desired to muzzle federal power in order to avoid some future emancipation law, Floyd was almost totally preoccupied with economic concerns in the summer of 1831. He was afraid that the tariff, the distribution plan, and other federal measures might impede his grandiose schemes and inhibit Virginia's commercial expansion.

As for slavery itself, Floyd was something of a maverick among Southern state leaders. Though an implacable Southern-rights man, the governor was a foe of the peculiar institution. In fact, he wanted slavery to be gradually abolished in Virginia and all the blacks colonized somewhere else, leaving the Old Dominion an unadulterated white man's paradise. Convinced in his own mind that slavery was a wasteful labor system that retarded commercial growth, Floyd opposed human bondage strictly out of economic considerations. Still, the recent state constitutional convention had refused to take up emancipation and colonization, so that slavery seemed more entrenched in Floyd's Virginia than ever. Thus for now Floyd could do nothing about the peculiar institution but live with it.

Meanwhile he had his plans and projects. Nothing could be done today, since it was Sunday, but tomorrow it was back to work for the governor. Tomorrow he was to see the Board of Public Works about the Northwest Turnpike Company. He was anxious to complete all the turnpikes and river and harbor improvements now under way, anxious to ensure "the future grandeur of the Common-wealth," to guide Virginia into a golden new era of boom and prosperity.[1]

Sunday morning, August 21, was sunny and hot down in Southampton County, too. At the Francis farm, twenty-six-year-old Nathaniel had already made his rounds and was now getting ready for church. A hardworking six-footer with thick eyebrows, full sideburns, and a stern mouth, Nathaniel in many ways was typical of the rural citizens of Southampton County. He did not have the time or the inclination to think deeply or read many books. He did not question the values and institutions of his slaveowning world, but accepted them as they were, and set himself to the task of making money and becoming a success. He ran the old home estate, consisting of some 360 acres, and had recently bought an additional 430 acres from John Reese. He had enough money to engage an overseer named Henry Doyle to manage his fifteen slaves—among them Sam and a strange, powerful individual named Will. Sam, for his part, had become quite a chum of Nat Turner these days . . . not that it bothered Nathaniel, for he liked Preacher Nat, had known him since boyhood, and allowed him the unheard-of privilege of referring to Nathaniel without the customary "Mr." In fact, Nathaniel was hardly "a mean son-of-a-bitch" and "a nigger breaker," as one writer has characterized him, because six free blacks voluntarily resided on his farm.

Around eight or nine that morning, the Francis family climbed into Nathaniel's carriage and set out for church. In the back sat Francis's two nephews—aged eight and three—who'd come to live at the farm as his charges. In front were his mother and his nineteen-year-old wife, Lavinia. About eight months pregnant with their first child, she was a rather pretty girl, with short hair, high cheekbones, and a wide and gentle mouth.[2]

Several miles to the south, Joseph Travis and his family were also on their way to church. Usually they attended Turner's Meeting House, where they were members, but no services were scheduled there today, so they were going down to Barnes's Church. Sally rode with Joseph in the front of the carriage; in the back were Putnam Moore and Joel Westbrook, a fourteen-year-old apprentice who boarded at the Travis place and worked in Joseph's wheelwright shop. Evidently Travis no longer employed an overseer, so the family slaves stayed behind without supervision. Their blacks didn't need watching—especially Nat. Travis thought him about the smartest, best-behaved slave a man was likely to own in all the county.

After church, the Travis family planned to visit some friends and relatives and would not come home until after dark. As they rode along the forested path, all dressed in their Sunday finest, birds chortled in the trees. There was hardly a cloud in the sky.[3]

It was later that same Sunday, deep in the woods near the Travis house at a place called Cabin Pond. In the sweltering noonday heat, Nat's lieutenants sat around a crackling fire, feasting on roast pig and apple brandy that Hark had filched that morning. All around them were towering cypress trees and water oaks, whose tangled limbs obscured the sun and cast the forest in moving shadows. The woods were alive with chattering insects and fluttering birds, and from the distance there came the occasional bark of dogs—slaves out trapping or hunting most likely. Here and there in the trees were pools of mud and water, with lily pads floating on the surface.

Swatting away flies and mosquitoes, the slaves talked freely around the campfire, certain that nobody had seen them enter the woods. Like the Travis and Francis families, most whites in the neighborhood were away at church and planned to picnic or visit the rest of the day, so that the slaves were free from supervision until Monday morning. From time to time, Nelson Williams piled wood on the smoking embers. Henry and Sam shared a jug of brandy while Hark Travis—muscular and intelligent—analyzed various plans they might adopt against the white man. To devise a plan and to share a final meal together were the reasons Nat had called them here.

The Prophet had not yet arrived. But two new recruits were present—Jack Reese and Will Francis. The property of William Reese, Jack was a hesitant, obsequious fellow who had little stomach for violence. But Hark, his brother-in-law, had dragged him here in spite of his reluctance to fight. As for Will, nothing is known about him beyond the fact that he belonged to Nathaniel Francis and was an expert axman with a sure killer's instinct. One writer claims that inordinate white cruelties had made him a killer, that he had seen a cherished wife sold off to a Negro trader and had been beaten so often that his back was covered with scars. The same chronicler states that a great scar ran from Will's right eye to his chin, which proved that he lived with "a mean master." In truth, these claims are almost entirely fictional: the available records say nothing about Will's physical appearance, his background, or his family (if he had a family). While Will may well have had a vicious master before Nathaniel, it seems impossible that young Francis would have beaten him so cruelly. For lack of evidence, Will is apt to remain a controversial figure who, out of unrecorded agonies and resentments under bondage, became a violent individual prepared to retaliate with extreme brutality.[4]

Around midafternoon, with tensions building at Cabin Pond, Nat made a dramatic lone-hand appearance—a move calculated to make him seem even more mysterious and mystical to his followers. Wearing an old hat, his huge, deep-set eyes ablaze from fasting and prayer, Nat appeared the very picture of brooding self-confidence this Sunday afternoon. His fierce eyes, broad shoulders, and brisk knock-kneed walk made him seem larger than he was. At thirty years old, Nat stood around five feet seven and weighed about 150 pounds. He now wore a mustache and cultivated a tuft of whiskers on his chin. He was a striking man, this coal-black Prophet, with his whiskers, moody expressions, and trembling, articulate voice.

He saluted his men as he came up—only to notice Jack and Will among them. Nat trusted Jack, who he knew was "only a tool in the hands of Hark." But the Prophet had doubts about Will. "How come you're here?" Nat demanded. Will replied that his life was worth no more than the others and that his liberty was just as dear to him. So you think to win your freedom? Nat asked. Will said he would get it or die in the attempt. That put him in full confidence, the Prophet decided, and Will stayed.

In the glare of pine-knot torches, they now made their plans. They would rise that night and "kill all the white people." They knew that Sunday night was the best time to strike, for whites would be tired and lulled after a day of visiting and drinking. Moreover, slaves habitually hunted on Sunday night—especially during August, the month of "jubilee" when most of the crops had been laid by and the blacks had relatively minor chores to do until picking time. So on Sunday nights white people expected a lot of clamor and commotion in the woods. Also, many whites in the militia were away at a Camp Meeting, so that Nat expected to encounter only minimal military resistance. The insurrection, he declared, would be so swift and so terrible that the whites would be too panic-stricken to fight back. Until they had sufficient recruits and equipment, the insurgents would annihilate everybody in their path— women and children included.

But Jack Reese objected to the scheme, complaining that "their number was too few." There were only seven of them, after all. How could seven men carry out such devastation? Nat was quick to reassure him. The Prophet had deliberately avoided an extensive plot that involved explicit plans and a lot of slaves. He knew that blacks had "frequently attempted similar things," but their plans had "leaked out." Nat intended for his revolt to happen without warning. "The march of destruction," he explained, "should be the first news of the insurrection," whereupon slaves and free blacks alike would rally to his banners. For months now his lieutenants had been spreading disaffection through the slave community, and he was confident that scores of Negroes would rise at the first word that General Nat was in their neighborhood. Then they would smash their way into Jerusalem, a connotation scarcely lost on the Prophet, and thus gain control of all Southampton County. He did not say what their ultimate objective was, but possibly he wanted to fight his way into the Dismal Swamp some twenty miles to the east. This immense, snake-filled quagmire had long been a haven for fugitives, and Nat may have planned to establish a slave stronghold there from which to launch punitive raids against Virginia and North Carolina. On the other hand, as he took his men aside now and exhorted them individually, he may have had no objective in mind beyond the extermination of every white on the ten-mile route to Jerusalem. There are indications that Nat expected God to guide him after the insurrection began, just as the Almighty had directed the prophets of old in their bloody, Bible-day wars.[5] Certainly Nat's command of unremitting carnage was that of Jehovah, who said through Ezekiel that His mighty wrath was on Jerusalem, whose people had disobeyed the Lord's statutes and transformed His judgments into the most terrible wickedness. They had come to worship false gods and had filled the land with violence, provoking Jehovah to punish them with a divine fury. Already God had visited them with pestilence and famine. Now the Almighty gave His injunctions through the prophet Ezekiel: "Go through the midst of the city, through the midst of Jerusalem, and set a mark upon the foreheads of the men that sigh and that cry for all the abominations that be done in the midst thereof." And the others in Jerusalem? "Go ye after him through the city, and smite," Jehovah thundered: "let not your eye spare, neither have ye pity: Slay utterly old and young, both maids, and little children, and women: but come not near any man upon whom is the mark; and begin at my sanctuary. . . . Defile the house, and fill the courts with the slain: go ye forth. And they went forth, and slew in the city."

It was sometime after midnight. With a slight wind murmuring in the darkness, the slaves set out by the light of a torch, moving through the woods toward the Travis farm—the first target in their holy war against the white man. They would spare Giles Reese, his wife and children, undoubtedly because Nat's own family lived on the Reese farm. Sometime in the previous week, Nat had seen his wife and had given her his sacred papers—the list of followers, the drawings of the crucifix and the sun.

Presently the insurgents emerged from the woods, extinguished the torch, and made their way across hedgerows and cotton patches—the very cotton patches Nat had toiled in for nine long years. The buildings of the Travis farm lay ahead, silhouetted against the night sky.

A couple of slaves—Austin and young Moses—greeted the insurgents as they came into the Travis yard. It was now around 2 A.M. on Monday, and the farm was deathly quiet. In the darkness the slaves gathered around the cider press and all drank except Nat. According to Moses, Nat then enjoined a couple of the insurgents "to make good their valiant boastings, so often repeated, of what they would do." Armed with axes, they moved across the yard to the house. Hark started to break the front door down, but Nat restrained him—the racket might wake the neighbors. Hark then placed a ladder against the house and Nat, carrying a hatchet, climbed up and disappeared through a second-story window. In a moment, he unbarred the door and whispered to his men, "The work is now open to you." They spread inside without a sound. The others wanted Nat the Prophet, Nat the black messiah, to strike the first blow and kill Joseph Travis. With Will close behind, Nat entered the master bedroom and made his way to the bed where Joseph and Sally lay sleeping. *Now.* Nat swung his hatchet in the darkness—a wild blow that glanced off Travis's head. Instantly Joseph bolted upright and screamed for his wife in deranged, incomprehensible terror. But Will moved in and hacked Joseph and Sally both to pieces, bringing his ax down again, and again, and again. In minutes Will and the others had slaughtered the four whites they found in the house, including Joel Westbrook and Putnam Moore. With the deaths of Putnam and Joseph Travis, Nat had no earthly masters left. After thirty years in bondage, he was free at last. *Yes, free at last.*

The rebels gathered up a handful of old muskets and followed General Nat out to the barn. There Nat paraded his men about, leading them through every military maneuver he knew to discipline them for the battles ahead. Not all of them, however, were proud of their work. Young Moses was extremely reluctant to leave the farm; they had to make him go. Meanwhile Jack Reese sank to his knees, his head in his hands, and said he was too sick to continue. But Hark made him get up and forced him along as they set out across the fields to Sal Francis's place. Along the way somebody remembered the Travis baby. Will and Henry returned and killed the child in its cradle.[6]

And so it went throughout that malignant night as the insurgents took farm after farm by surprise. They lured Sal Francis from his one-room cabin, and Will and Sam fell on him in the yard, cutting and clubbing him to death while his dogs raged and his slaves ran about in mute confusion. At Mrs. Piety Reese's place, the rebels found the house unlocked and killed Mrs. Reese and her son William. As William, Jack's master, lay in a mangled heap, Jack seemed to overcome his squeamishness: he put on a pair of William's socks and shoes, stepped over his body, and joined the other insurgents after they had cut up Reese's overseer (though he survived, the man was to be maimed for the rest of his life).

So far everything was going as Nat had planned. In order not to arouse the countryside, the slaves had used no firearms, instead stabbing and decapitating their victims. Although they confiscated horses, weapons, and brandy, they took mainly what they needed to continue the struggle, and there were no rapes—Nat helped see to that. Nat now carried a light dress sword, but for some mysterious reason (a fatal irresolution? the dread again?) he had killed nobody yet.

Just before sunrise the insurgents reached Wiley Francis's plantation, some two miles south of Mrs. Reese's. Suddenly Nat halted his men, for something had moved in Wiley's house. Then a voice sounded from inside—it was Wiley's voice. "Here I am, boys; I will not go from my home to be killed!" According to a white chronicler, some of Wiley's slaves moved into the yard and vowed to fight the rebels if they came any closer. To avoid a lot of noise that might alarm the neighborhood, Nat led his men off, supposedly remarking that Wiley Francis wasn't worth killing anyway. They hurried on now, passing a stagnant pond with clouds of insects swirling across the surface, and made their way to Elizabeth Turner's farm just as day was breaking. For Nat it was a kind of homecoming, for he had lived at the Turner place until Samuel's death and had worked in the surrounding fields for a decade. Though still a widow, Elizabeth was getting along fairly well: she employed an overseer and owned eighteen slaves. Nat had known some of them all his life.

At the gate Nat gave the signal and the slaves stormed the buildings in a rush, overrunning the still, where they shot and killed Hartwell Peebles, the overseer, and then charged across the yard to the house. Will broke the door down with a single blow of his ax. Inside, in the middle of the room, too frightened to move or cry out,

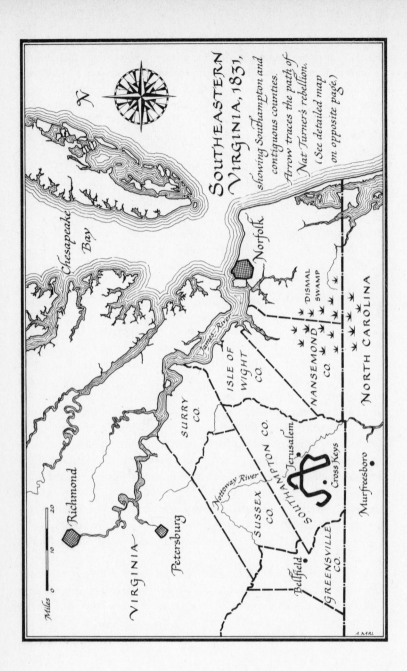

SOUTHEASTERN VIRGINIA, 1831, showing Southampton and contiguous counties. Arrow traces the path of Nat Turner's rebellion. (See detailed map on opposite page.)

A. KARL

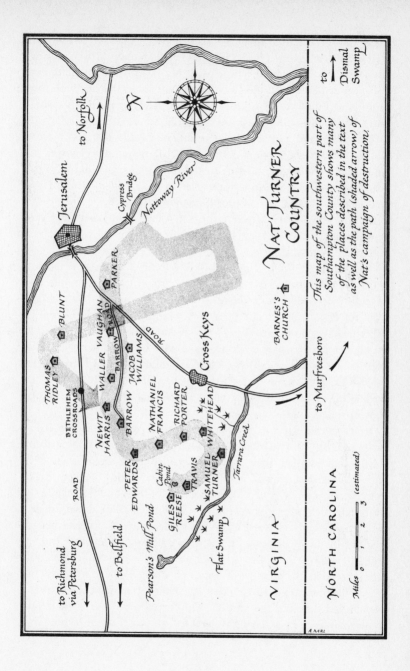

to Richmond
via Petersburg

to Bellfield

Pearson's Mill Pond

ROAD

BLUNT

THOMAS
RIDLEY

BETHLEHEM
CROSSROADS

NEWIT
HARRIS

WALLER VAUGHAN

PETER
EDWARDS

BARROW

ROAD

JACOB
WILLIAMS

NATHANIEL
FRANCIS

PARKER

Cabin
Pond

GILES
REESE

TRAVIS

RICHARD
PORTER

Cross Keys

SAMUEL
WHITEHEAD

Flat Swamp

Tarrara Creek

to Murfreesboro

BARNES'S
CHURCH

VIRGINIA

NORTH CAROLINA

Miles   0 1 2 3   (estimated)

Jerusalem

to Norfolk

Cypress
Bridge

Nottoway River

N

to
Dismal
Swamp

NAT TURNER
COUNTRY

This map of the southwestern part of
Southampton County shows many
of the places described in the text
as well as the path (shaded arrow) of
Nat's campaign of destruction.

A. NARI

73

stood Elizabeth and a neighbor named Mrs. Newsom. While Will attacked Elizabeth with his ax, the Prophet took Mrs. Newsom's hand and hit her over the head with his sword. But the blade was dull and evidently he could not bring himself to kill her with anything else. Finally Will moved Nat aside and chopped Mrs. Newsom to death as methodically as though he were cutting wood.

After they had ransacked the house, Nat enlisted a few recruits among his old slave companions. Davy Turner, however, did not want to go; the insurgents threatened to kill him if he didn't. Then Joe Harris—a new recruit—went over to the distillery where Hartwell Peebles lay and put on the white man's clothes.[7]

By now there were fifteen insurgents—nine on horses—and they were armed with a motley assortment of guns, axes, swords, clubs, and hoes. With the sun low in the east, Hark took a group on foot to another farm while Nat and Will led the horsemen northeastward toward Turner's Meeting House, through the same woods and swamps Nat had romped in as a boy. In a moment they emerged from the forests and kicked their horses across the fields to Catherine Whitehead's plantation. Caty Whitehead was another widow, a prominent lady known all over the county both for her hospitality and for her pretty daughters—especially Margaret and Harriet. Her son Richard, a young Methodist preacher, also lived with her. Yesterday, down at Barnes's Church, he had exhorted a congregation that included the Travis family.

Pious young Richard was in the cotton patch when the insurgents rode up in a swirl of dust. They could see him talking to his slaves and pointing their way. Will called Richard over—and he came, though reluctantly. Yes? he asked. What did they want? The executioner, as Nat styled Will, took his ax to Whitehead while the other rebels chanted, *"Kill him!" "Kill him!"* Falling down under a cedar tree, trying to ward off Will's slashing ax, Whitehead begged Nat for his life. "Please," he wept, "why do you want to kill me?" But Nat showed the white preacher no mercy—and neither did Will, who shredded the man with windmill blows. When Will was finished, the insurgents surrounded the house, but not before several people had fled into the garden. Nat chased after one of them, but it turned out to be a slave girl, as terrified as any of the whites, and he let her go. All around him, all over the Whitehead place, there were scenes of unspeakable violence, as the rebels butchered three of the Whitehead girls and a grandchild. Nat saw Will drag Caty Whitehead kicking and screaming out of the house and almost sever her head from her body. Two of her slaves—Jack and Andrew —ran away from the plantation, away into the woods. The other twenty-five or so Negroes, many of them children, stood rooted to their spots around the sheds, cabins, and barns. From the garden, Nat could see where tentacles of ivy crawled up the side of the house, whose windows resembled the eyes of a skull. Figures came and went in those windows—Nat's men yelling at one another and banging around inside in search of Margaret and Harriet. Now an old man's voice rose above the clamor: it was a family servant called Old Hubbard, yammering on about how they wasn't in here, nobody in here (Hubbard was lying—he had hidden Miss Harriet between the bed and the mat in one of the bedrooms). In a moment Nat ran around the outside of the house, only to come upon Margaret Whitehead hiding under a cellar cap between two chimneys. Miss Margaret ran crying for her life. Though he scarcely knew the girl, Nat set out after her—a wild chase against the hot August sun. With his men and the Whitehead slaves watching up at the Big House, Nat overtook the girl in a field and hit her again and again with his sword, but she would not die. In desperation he picked up a fence rail and beat her to death. Finally he had killed someone.

Back at the house, Nat asked where Jack and Andrew were, only to find out from Hubbard that they had run off. Then the Prophet beseeched a couple of other male slaves to ride with him, but they refused. They were afraid—afraid of the white man's reprisals, the whips, chains, the hangman's noose. And they recoiled from Nat's own brand of violence—the beatings and decapitations. So, no, they would not go with him this time.

In a moment two other slaves rode up with a dead raccoon. They had been out hunting in the forest, heard all the commotion at the Whitehead plantation, and come to investigate. And now, looking around, they knew grimly what it was all about. One of the slaves belonged to the Edwin Turner estate and was named Nat, like the Prophet. The other was Joe and was the property of John Clark

Turner. The Prophet took them aside and talked to them intently. They shook their heads, seemed to hesitate, and then nodded in solemn agreement. They would go with him.

Hark arrived with the infantry, reporting that they had slain Henry Bryant and his family. At that, Nat and his lieutenants held a war council in the Whitehead yard, cluttered now with human wreckage. Nat, drawing lines in the dirt, declared that the infantry would proceed in this direction and get Howell Harris and Trajan Doyle. Meanwhile he and the cavalry would strike Richard Porter and Nathaniel Francis. Then with additional recruits the columns would reunite and drive on to Jerusalem.

After the insurgents had gone, Jack and Andrew returned to the Whitehead plantation. They were "much disturbed and greatly grieved," Old Hubbard observed, as they described how they had run blindly from farm to farm, only to return. They didn't know where else to go. When Hubbard said that General Nat wanted them to follow, they became even more distressed. Should they go? Should they stay? Finally they mounted the same horse, told Hubbard they were going after Nat because they didn't know what else to do, and sauntered off into the woods.

At once Hubbard ran into the house and found Harriet alive but in a state of shock. He hid her in the forest and then returned to the house for food and bedding. In her distraught condition, though, Harriet feared that Old Hubbard had gone to fetch the insurgents —the sound of plunging hooves? of voices in the wind? She made her way deeper into the woods and concealed herself again, refusing to answer Hubbard's cries, refusing to come back to the house. At last some white men found her, muddy, bruised, and mosquito bitten, and took her down to Cross Keys, where she shocked people with the grisly details of her story.[8]

From the Whitehead place, Nat led his horsemen along a forested path toward Richard Porter's small plantation. The Prophet bypassed John Clark Turner's house, electing to spare his old boyhood chum in spite of his own command that all whites in their path should be exterminated. In open fields now, the riders kicked their horses and mules faster and faster, until at last they raced down the lane to Porter's house, scattering dogs and chickens as they went. But the Porters had fled—forewarned by their own slaves that a revolt was under way. In fact, the initial alarm had come from slaves who'd witnessed the Travis and Sal Francis massacres. And other Negroes had carried the news to the Porter neighborhood.

Nat, of course, was dismayed that some of his own people had betrayed him, dismayed that the flames of rebellion did not burn in the heart of every slave. Well, the alarm was spreading now, the available militia would soon be mobilizing, so he told Will to take the horsemen on while he retrieved the infantry. They would meet again in the Francis vicinity. At that Nat rode off in one direction and Will and the cavalry in another.

Presently Jack and Andrew Whitehead rode up to the Porter house on their single horse. They asked a slave named Venus, "Did the Negroes come and kill your white people?" No, Venus replied, her white folks had been warned about the Negroes and had all fled into the woods. Jack and Andrew were in a terrible fret. General Nat's *orders,* they exclaimed to Venus, so what else could they do? They kicked their horse—kicked and kicked it—and set out slowly after the insurgents.

As was his habit on work days, Nathaniel Francis rose at dawn that Monday and went out to inspect his crops and pungent stock pens. There was a sharp aroma of cedar logs and rough-hewn timber in the air, and the wind was blowing across the corn like the breath of an oven. After his rounds, Nathaniel enjoyed a hearty breakfast with his family—eggs and lean bacon, most likely, with grits, hot bread, and preserves—and then conferred with Doyle about the day's work.

At about eight that morning, a Negro boy came running down the lane, yelling and stammering incomprehensibly. Nathaniel recognized him as one of Sally's slaves, from the Travis farm two or three miles to the southwest. "Some folks," the boy blurted out, "some folks have killed all the white folks." Young Francis laughed at him. "You don't know what you're talking about." But something about the boy—the fear etched on his face—alarmed Nathaniel. Hurrying back to the house, he told the women about the boy and said he was going down to Sally's to investigate. After he had ridden off, Nathaniel's mother became extremely upset—after all Sally was her daughter—and took a bypath that led to the Travis farm. Lavinia, eight months pregnant, remained behind with Doyle, Nathaniel's two nephews, and all the slaves except Will and Sam. Nobody seemed to know where they were.

As Nathaniel and his mother moved toward the southwest, Will and the insurgent cavalry approached the Francis farm from the southeast. Francis's three-year-old nephew, oblivious to the slaves' guns and axes, ran up the lane to greet Will and Sam Francis. Will decapitated the child with his ax. The other nephew, watching from a clump of weeds in the barnyard, screamed involuntarily, whereupon a couple of slaves rode over and cut him down as well.

By now the farm was in pandemonium, as the Francis slaves scurried about the sheds and cabins and Doyle ran yelling into the house. In a moment he came back out—and the slaves shot him dead. Will and Sam then ran inside the Big House crying for Nathaniel. But the house servants said he wasn't here, said he and his mother both had gone down to Mistress Sally's. And a slave named Nelson claimed that Lavinia had also escaped. (But Lavinia had not escaped—Nelson had concealed her in an upstairs cuddy, where she had fainted from all the screams and gunshots.) After a fruitless search, the two insurgents dashed outside, only to spot a white woman standing in the lane with her child. It was Mrs. Williams, the wife of a local schoolteacher named John "Choctaw" Williams. The teacher was called Choctaw because he was dark-skinned and wore his hair long like an Indian. After he had left for school, his wife and child had come to spend the day at the Francis farm . . . and now stood immobilized in the lane, unable to comprehend the sight of black men running toward them with axes.

After killing Mrs. Williams and her child, the insurgents gathered at the brandy still and celebrated in noisy jubilation. Then they enlisted slave reinforcements: Dred Francis came voluntarily, but three teenage boys—the oldest was about fifteen and "very badly grown"—had to be forced along like hostages. A slave later testified that the boys all rode the same horse and "were constantly guarded by negroes with guns who were ordered to shoot them if they attempted to escape." According to white chroniclers, another Francis slave refused to leave the farm, so the rebels sliced his heel strings to keep him from alerting the neighbors.

Inside the house, Lavinia regained consciousness at about the time the slaves rode off. When she came out of her hideaway, she found a couple of servants fighting over her clothes. One of them, a girl named Charlotte, attacked Lavinia with a dirk knife, but loyal slaves pulled Charlotte away. With Nelson's help, Lavinia left the farm and made her way down to the Travis place, passing the very woods where Nat rode about in search of his infantry. At the Travis house were a couple of white men who were stunned and sickened by the spectacle inside. One of them took Lavinia to a nearby hill where her mother-in-law and a number of wives and children were huddled in inert terror. Where was Nathaniel? Lavinia asked. Was he alive? Was he all right? Mrs. Francis said he had left her here and joined an armed party; she didn't know where he was now. Soon a flock of sheep came up the trail, and the women, mistaking the noise for a slave army, scattered into the swamps. The two Francis women also took flight, heading southeast toward Cross Keys.

Meanwhile, some two miles away, Choctaw Williams had heard cries from the direction of Caty Whitehead's plantation and had gone to see what the commotion was about. What he found there was beyond belief. He interrogated Caty's slaves, mostly women and children, who babbled on about how armed Negroes were decapitating everybody in sight and pressing into their ranks all the slave men they could find. Williams hurried back toward his house, only to come across some Negro boys along the path. "Your family's been killed," one said, "at the Francis place." And Williams found them there—his child beheaded and his wife hacked to pieces. Almost demented from shock, Williams mounted a horse and raced southward toward Murfreesboro, North Carolina, the headquarters of the Governor's Guards.[9]

Will's cavalry exploded out of the woods as though shot from a cannon, and charged across the fields toward Peter Edwards's elegant home, rising ahead of them in a sea of corn. With his impressive house and twenty-nine slaves, Edwards was a prominent man in the area and so a prime target for Will's ax this day. But to his disappointment the Edwards family too had escaped. The rebels had to move fast now, lest any more whites get away. After recruiting an Edwards slave named Sam, Will led the cavalry out across the meadow in front of the house and down the forested path beyond.

At last the riders came to John Barrow's farm, situated on a wooded knoll at the head of the Barrow Road, itself a strategic objective in the rebellion. The only bona fide road in this part of the county, it ran eastward for about five miles until it intersected the main highway from Murfreesboro to Jerusalem.

Old man Barrow, a veteran of the War of 1812, was hoeing in his cotton patch as the slaves approached. He had heard rumors about a slave uprising in the backwoods northwest of Cross Keys, but had dismissed them as preposterous. Now, with Will's cavalry bearing down on him, Barrow could scarcely believe his eyes. He stood his ground, though, and fought the blacks hand-to-hand while his wife fled out of their house. Later she testified that one of her servants—a woman named Lucy—tried to stop her in the garden, but somehow Mrs. Barrow got away. Her husband was not so lucky, for the insurgents overwhelmed him and slit his throat. As a tribute to his courage, they wrapped his body in a quilt and left a plug of tobacco on his chest. After they had gone, another Negro saw Lucy and Moses Barrow take four pieces of Barrow's silver and hide the money in a feather bag under a handkerchief.

Meanwhile, back in the Francis and Porter neighborhood, Nat had finally located the footmen under Hark. Although they had slain a white man, the slaves had found another farm deserted—proof that the cry of insurrection was in the wind. Moreover, several recruits had gotten lost in all the confusion and were now thrashing about somewhere in between Nat's two columns. In desperation the Prophet ordered Hark to bring the infantry on the run and then set out alone after the horsemen. For a time Nat rode chaotically through the countryside, chasing after one column and then the other, almost always reaching the farms after his scattered forces had done the killing and gone. At length he passed through old man Barrow's place—yes, Will had been here all right—and then headed down the Barrow Road into the eastern sun. Finally, at about 9:30 A.M., the Prophet found both columns waiting for him at

Captain Newit Harris's plantation. The slaves shouted and waved their weapons when Nat rode up, his horse lathered in sweat. For no matter how indecisive he may have seemed in hand-to-hand combat, Nat was still their leader—still their holy man—and to them his brooding presence was a thrilling spectacle. Nat saluted his cheering troops, but he could not have been happy at what he saw: the insurgents had pillaged the house (the Harris family had escaped before they arrived) and had scattered furniture and clothing about the yard. Several slaves had invaded the brandy cellar and carried the barrels out to the yard, broken them open with axes, and were now sitting around in drunken reverie. Nat ordered his men to stand at attention and apparently gave them a pep talk. They were forty strong now and all mounted. Many of the recruits had joined up eager indeed to kill all the white people. But the Francis boys, Moses Travis, and Davy Turner still had to be guarded. And Jack and Andrew Whitehead, who had finally over-taken the insurgents on their single horse, were still visibly confused and distressed.

As Nat harangued his men, a slave stepped forward to challenge the Prophet. The man was Aaron Harris, a Negro overseer at the Harris plantation. He tried to dissuade the blacks from going on, arguing that they did not have a chance against the white man's powerful forces. But Nat cut in on him. There were only eighty thousand whites in the country, the Prophet told his followers, and they could easily be crushed if enough slaves rallied to his banners. But Aaron emphatically disagreed. In the War of 1812 he had served with his master as a body servant. The insurgents, he de-clared, would understand how hopeless their revolt was if they "had seen as many white people as he saw in Norfolk." But Nat, em-ploying all his remarkable gifts of oratory, kept his men at his side. With a cry, he ordered them to mount up and move out the Barrow Road toward Jerusalem.

As they rode, Nat and his lieutenants—Hark, Nelson, Henry, Sam, and Will—held a horseback war council. They were in Nelson's neighborhood now; and since he was a leader among the slaves in the area, Nat expected a number of them to enlist in his crusade. But with the element of surprise gone they had to devise new tactics. Accordingly Nat placed his twenty most dependable fighters in front and sent them galloping down on the homesteads before anybody could escape. The rest of his troops moved helter-skelter behind the advance cavalry, some guarding the Negro hostages, others drinking brandy. For some unknown reason, Nat stationed himself in the rear of his strung-out forces, riding alone again, lost in his thoughts and his prayers.[10]

By midmorning on Monday, Southampton's slave grapevine was buzzing with stories about ructions and wars. Some reports had it that the British were in the area, others that General Nat himself had finally risen. The slaves at Ben Blunt's homestead watched as a white man galloped by, crying that "the negroes are behind killing the white people." One slave turned to another and said, "Ah: didn't I tell you there would be a war?" At Benjamin Edwards's place, several Negroes gathered in a newly cleared field to relish the news. Among them was Barry Newsom, a free Negro apprenticed to Peter Edwards; he and a couple of male slaves said they were going to find General Nat. When a free black woman tried to dissuade them, one "made light" of the news "and said it was nothing and ought to have been done long ago—that the negroes had been punished long enough."

Meanwhile, off to the west, on a plantation in neighboring Greensville County, a slave girl encountered a Negro man off the side of the road: he was jumping up and down and kicking his heels. Hadn't he heard? the girl cried. The British had invaded Southampton County and were murdering people there. Wasn't the man afraid? No, he was not afraid. If they came here, he said joyfully, he would join them and slit a few white throats himself. Then he would have as much money as his master.

Other slaves reacted to the rebellion with mixed emotions. There were blacks who loathed their condition and resented their masters, but who balked at killing them to redress their grievances. And all about the county, in fields and sheds alike, there were slaves who were confused, uncertain, and afraid—afraid of the white man's vengeance, afraid of the unknown. And, alas, there were many slaves like Hubbard and Nelson, who felt an ineradicable loyalty to their masters and sought to protect them from violence.

When whites first heard about the troubles, some actually thought that another war with England had begun and that British troops really were in Southampton. But by nine or so that morning, whites had established that an insurrection was under way, and church bells began tolling the alarm all through the backwoods. As Nat's little army moved along the Barrow Road, white families rushed to Jerusalem by wagon and horseback, throwing the county seat into bedlam. Soon church bells clanged in Jerusalem, too, and shouting men rode through the countryside in a desperate effort to fetch the scattered militiamen. Meanwhile, Jerusalem citizens barricaded the bridge across the Nottoway River, scanning the Murfreesboro road for a sign of the slave army, said to be five hundred strong. As waves of hysteria washed through the town, women and children locked themselves in stores and churches, whose bells tolled on through the sweltering day.

In all the commotion, Justice James Trezevant of the Southampton County Court managed to scribble off a message which an express rider would carry up to Petersburg and Richmond. The note warned that a terrible insurrection had blazed up in Southampton and that several families had been obliterated. Send us arms and men at once, the note said: a large military force may be needed to crush the revolt. Stuffing the note in his pocket, the express rider galloped across the bridge and headed west, a lone figure receding down the road to Bellfield and Petersburg.[11]

It was a hot, lazy summer morning for Levi Waller, proprietor of one of the larger homesteads along the Barrow Road. His farm, which contained blacksmith and wheelwright shops as well as the inevitable distillery, served as a meeting place and a community center for his neighborhood. Beyond the main house were the usual rickety cabins, which Waller's eighteen slaves made their homes. About a quarter of a mile away was a boarding school, attended by Waller's younger children. The school was open the year round and was operated by William Crocker.

Around 10 A.M., while Waller was at the distillery, somebody came to his place with a disturbing report. "The negroes have risen," the messenger exclaimed, "and are murdering the whites and are *coming*." Alarmed, Waller sent his son to alert the school and get his children. His son returned with Crocker and several other children as well. "Go to the house and load the guns," Waller shouted to Crocker. But in a moment the teacher ran back to the still, crying that the slaves "were in sight."

Before Waller could arm himself, Nat's advance horsemen swept into the yard, a whirlwind of swords and axes. A small girl escaped by crawling up a dirt chimney, scarcely daring to breathe as the blacks chased down her screaming schoolmates. Waller himself dived over a rail fence and burrowed into some tall weeds. In a moment, an armed slave rode up to the fence only a few yards from where Waller lay. It was Dred Francis—Waller "knew him well." After scanning the weeds for what seemed an eternity, Dred turned back to the house, where the other insurgents were busily decapitating the white children.

Incredibly enough, Waller witnessed many of the killings, for he stole back to the farmhouse and concealed himself in an orchard nearby. As he looked on in horror, the rebels slashed his wife to death and beheaded two of his daughters. Afterward, he noticed Sam Edwards standing alone and "wiping his eyes" while the others drank copiously from a brandy barrel. Among them was Albert, one of Waller's own slaves.

Then Waller saw a small, hunched-over Negro ride up. To his astonishment, he recognized the horseman as Nat Turner, the innocuous mystic, wearing an old hat and carrying a silver sword. Nat took charge at once, broke up the drinking party, and ordered tearful Sam Edwards to "get on your horse." Sam "seemed not disposed to get up," Waller noted, but Nat made him do it. As the slaves prepared to go, another of Waller's Negroes—a man called Yellow Davy—appeared in the yard. He was "dressed clean," Waller later testified, and was called "brother *Clements*" by one of the insurgents. He drank with them, rode Waller's own horse, and followed Nat out to the road "in great glee." There Nat shouted, "Go ahead," and once again the advance cavalry thundered away. The other insurgents moved off in considerable confusion, with Nat again bringing up the rear.

Inconsolable with grief, Waller fled into the woods and swamps. The little girl in the chimney also got away, as did two of Waller's sons and Crocker, the schoolmaster.[12]

By now two columns of armed whites had organized and were moving in cautious pursuit of the slave army. One sortie, numbering thirty or forty men, marched under William C. Parker, a veteran of the War of 1812 and a well-known Jerusalem lawyer in his late thirties. Parker's column picked up the insurgents' trail at Newit Harris's plantation and followed it to the Barrow Road, passing one assaulted homestead after another. "The blood," Parker later reported, "had hardly congealed" in the houses they visited.

Meanwhile a second party of some twenty men, brought together by Captain Arthur Middleton of the Southampton militia, moved along somewhere between Parker's column and the Negro insurgents (evidently the white parties were unaware of one another). Middleton's group reached Waller's place not fifteen minutes after the insurgents had raided it. What the whites found there made them retch: ten decapitated children piled in "one bleeding heap." Another mangled child was still alive; the volunteers placed her under a tree, but she soon died. Captain Middleton was so upset that he left for home to protect his own family. But eighteen others elected to continue—no matter the size or ferocity of the slave army—and set out under the command of Alexander P. Peete and James Bryant.

A short while later they found Albert Waller lying drunk in the road. To make certain he would not fight any more, they cut his heel strings. Some time afterward, a militia company from Greensville County came on the crippled man. "As a beneficial example to the other insurgents," one white said, the militia tied Albert to a tree and riddled him with bullets.[13]

As Nat's lieutenants raced along the Barrow Road, they found more and more homesteads deserted. General Nelson, worried lest his own master—Jacob Williams—get away, rode ahead while the insurgents attacked Bill Williams's farm. When Nelson reached the home place alone, Jacob was gone all right, but the other slaves expected him back soon. So Nelson donned his master's best clothes and waited for him in the yard. At about 11 A.M. Jacob arrived after tending to some business elsewhere in the neighborhood. Well, he was astonished to see Nelson in his own clothes and might have said something had the Negro not started toward him with a menacing gesture. At that, Jacob went off in the woods to measure timber—or so he claimed later. Somehow, he said, he did not understand that an insurrection was going on.

Nelson, meanwhile, went to a new field and tried to lure Caswell Worrell, the overseer, back to the house. But Worrell sensed that something was wrong—Nelson was terribly insolent—and refused to leave the field. It was a decision that saved his life.

Others at Jacob's farm were not so fortunate. An overseer from another homestead, preparing to load some corn at Jacob's barn, spotted Nat's advance horsemen in the lane. "Lord, who is that coming?" the overseer declared. And they were the last words he ever uttered, as the slaves rode the man down and disemboweled him. Then they killed Jacob's wife and three children, crashed through the timber to Worrell's cabin, and dispatched his family as well.

Back at the main buildings, Nelson entered the kitchen shed and met a slave named Cynthia. She noted that he was dressed "very clean" and seemed "very sick." He told her, "Cynthia, you do not know me. I do not know when you will see me again." Outside, he stepped over the bodies without any show of grief, Cynthia later testified, and rode away with the other insurgents.

Down the road now to widow Rebecca Vaughan's house. Somehow Rebecca had not heard about the revolt and was on the porch preparing lunch when she noticed horsemen coming up from the road. She thought it was her son, who was due about now with several fox hunters she planned to entertain. Her niece, an eighteen-year-old beauty named Anne Elizabeth, was upstairs primping for the male guests.

Only when the horsemen plunged into the yard did Rebecca recognize them as Negroes. With a cry, she hurried inside and bolted the door, but the slaves formed a circle around the house, shouted "imprecations," and aimed their guns at the doors and windows. Rebecca shut one of the windows—and then stood there pleading through the glass: "Please, take whatever you want, but don't kill us." An insurgent took careful aim, shot, and her face splintered in the windowpane.

Anne Elizabeth rushed downstairs just as some blacks broke the door down. They shot her, too, and flung her body into the yard, to bake under the sun. After butchering the overseer and Rebecca's other son, the rebels prevailed on an old Negro woman in the kitchen. They called for food and brandy, she recounted later, "and becoming nice, damned the brandy as vile stuff."

Some distance behind his troops, Nat rode alone in the sun, with crows and vultures already circling the homesteads his cavalry had assaulted. He came to Bill Williams's place, where the insurgents had slain Williams and his two children, then had made Mrs. Williams lie down beside her husband's corpse and had blasted her with muskets. And down the road a ways was Jacob Williams's farm with its macabre sights.

Why Nat remained in back of his troops, refusing to participate in the killings along the Barrow Road, is an enigma. Maybe he was planning strategies, objectives, alternatives (in case of strong white resistance). Maybe he was searching the blazing heavens for a sign . . . waiting for his God to appear . . . expecting the earth to shake and the forests to part with an ear-splitting roar all the way to Jerusalem.

On the other hand, Nat had been fasting for several days and may well have been too weak to try any more killing himself. Or maybe as God's Prophet he preferred to let Will and his other lieutenants do the actual slaughtering. It is also possible that this extraordinary man, in spite of all his rage and all his terrible sense of destiny, had for now lost the will to kill. Maybe what he'd done to Margaret Whitehead had sapped his strength and filled him with doubts. After all, that had been such an intimate act of destruction —beating the girl to death with his own hands. A loss of will then? The old dread again? We shall never know for certain. But the story of Ezekiel in the Old Testament may offer some insight. For as Ezekiel watched the slaughter in Biblical Jerusalem, he fell on his face and cried, "Ah Lord GOD! wilt thou destroy all the residue of Israel in thy pouring out of thy fury upon Jerusalem?"

Still, was the fury not justified? Nat was sitting on his horse in Rebecca Vaughan's yard, viewing the bodies there as he had studied other corpses in the wake of his advancing columns. He felt "a silent satisfaction," he declared later. And that was all he ever revealed about his feelings along the Barrow Road.[14]

Around noon on Monday the insurgents reached the Jerusalem highway, and Nat soon joined them. Behind them lay a zigzag path of unredeemable devastation: some fifteen homesteads sacked and approximately sixty whites slain. Still, the slaves had not waged indiscriminate warfare—Nat had spared several whites, including Giles Reese and John Clark Turner. And on the Barrow Road the Prophet had called his axmen back from one homestead, because he believed the poor white inhabitants "thought no better of themselves than they did of negroes." By now Nat's force amounted to sixty or seventy men—among them Barry Newsom, Billy Artis, and one or two other free Negroes. Artis, for his part, resided on a fourteen-acre farm on Rosa Swamp, near Benjamin Turner's old place. Perhaps because he had a slave wife and six children, Artis had been reluctant to join the insurrection. And even after he enlisted, some reports contend, he wept at all the savage killing. But he became inured to it and with a mechanical detachment began slaying whites himself.

If the rebels were to slay any more and attain their strategic objectives, they had to do something and fast. For even at its zenith the insurgent army showed signs of disintegration. A few reluctant slaves had already escaped or deserted. And many others were roaring drunk, so drunk they could scarcely ride their horses, let alone do any fighting. To make matters worse, many of the confiscated muskets were broken or too rusty to fire.

Nat resolved to march on Jerusalem at once and seize all the arms and ammunition he could find there. The town lay only two or three miles away, and as the rebels lurched forward they could see smoke rising over the trees and hear church bells tolling in the distance. But a half-mile up the road the Prophet stopped at James Parker's place, because some of his men had relatives and friends there who might join the rebellion. When the insurgents did not return, Nat rode the half-mile down to the house and found his men not in the slave cabins, but out in Parker's yard swilling brandy. Infuriated at their lack of discipline, the Prophet ordered them back to the road at once.

On the way back they met a party of armed men. Whites! This was the column of eighteen volunteers under Peete and Bryant; they had already routed Nat's small guard at the gate and were now advancing toward the Parker house. With renewed zeal, Nat rallied his remaining troops and ordered them into battle formation. Clearly this kind of warfare—a stand-up fight with an armed opponent— was more to his liking. As the whites approached, Captain Peete ordered them to hold their fire until within thirty paces. Suddenly a musket exploded in the white ranks and Peete's horse bolted forward, carrying the hapless captain straight through the Negro lines. In all the confusion, Nat saw some of the whites falling back. "Charge!" he cried. "Fire on them!" Yelling at the top of their lungs, wielding axes, clubs, and gun butts, the Negroes scrambled after the whites, knocking two down and chasing the rest back eastward into Parker's cornfield. Meanwhile, Captain Bryant's horse also stampeded and swept him away into the woods and out of the battle. But just when the slaves seemed about to win, their fortunes irrevocably changed. White reinforcements arrived, and more were on the way from nearby Jerusalem. Regrouping in the cornfield, the whites counterattacked, throwing the rebels back in much disorder. White marksmen killed Hark's mount, but Nat caught another for him with shot and musket balls whizzing by. In the fighting five or six of Nat's best men fell wounded, though none of them died. Several insurgents, too drunk to fight any more, staggered off into the woods and made their way home. Dred Francis, his arm shot away, stumbled through the rows of corn and also escaped.

Carrying their wounded with them, Nat and some sixteen other insurgents beat a horseback retreat into the dense forests along the Nottoway River, some three miles south of Jerusalem. If the Prophet had often seemed irresolute earlier in the revolt, he was now undaunted, as though he had tapped some hidden reservoir of strength. Even though his force was greatly reduced, he still wanted to storm Jerusalem. Clearly the main highway was blocked with militia— more than he had expected—but that was not the only way. He led his battered troops down a little-known back road, planning to cross the Cypress Bridge and strike Jerusalem from the rear. But when they reached the bridge and peered out of the underbrush, they found the place crawling with armed whites.

The insurgents were frightened now and desperate. What now,

Nat? They would head south, the Prophet decided, and gather additional recruits in Allen's quarter east of Cross Keys. But they must put an end to all the drinking. He and his lieutenants had worried about this from the outset, and their worries had been confirmed. The brandy was their worst foe—worse even than the white man—so no more of it. Leave the cider presses and brandy barrels alone.

Considerably sobered now, the rebels fell back south of Jerusalem and raided several more farms, only to find them deserted. At last they came to Mrs. John Thomas's farm, but she had fled in a carriage with her fifteen-year-old son, George H. Thomas, destined to become a celebrated Union general in the Civil War. The insurgents imprisoned some of the Thomas slaves, then struck out north again and headed back across the Jerusalem highway at the Barrow Road intersection, miraculously eluding all the scattered patrols out looking for them. William Parker's column tracked the slaves all day Monday, but "fortune seemed to sport with us," Parker said, "bringing us nearly together, and yet, making us pursue separate routes." As the insurgents rode toward the north, they came across several Negroes with inauspicious news: they had seen stragglers from Nat's force running through the woods back toward the Travis and Francis farms. Nat elected to push across the road that led to Bellfield and gather recruits at the Ridley plantations, two of the largest in the county. Then he would march back to his own neighborhood, rally his scattered followers, and storm down on Jerusalem a second time.

At dusk the blacks reached Thomas Ridley's plantation, hoping to enlist reinforcements among his 145 slaves—40 of them men. But the militia had barricaded the main buildings, ready to fight the rebels if they came there. So Nat led them out into the woods where they encamped for the night. Sometime after dark four of Ridley's slaves joined the Prophet, but that was all.

Still, Nat would not despair. With the recruits acquired that afternoon, his little army was back to forty men again. Tomorrow he would swell his ranks to seventy or eighty. Then they would smash their way into Jerusalem. This war was not over yet. God had not forsaken him. Tomorrow the battle would turn and victory would be theirs.

But for now the Prophet was tired, very tired. He needed to sleep for a while. He put out picket lines and then lay down in the brush. Tomorrow, somehow, victory would be theirs.[15]

All Monday night news of the insurrection spread beyond Southampton County as couriers raced along separate roads to Norfolk and Petersburg. When the express rider reached Petersburg with James Trezevant's communiqué, town authorities had considerable trouble deciphering and authenticating Trezevant's handwriting. Then they ordered Petersburg to go on the alert, and clanging bells shattered the stillness of the night. Soon volunteers mobilized at the courthouse and set out for Southampton with all the organization of a lynch mob.

Meanwhile another horseman carried Trezevant's message up to Richmond, arriving there around 3 A.M. on Tuesday. In his excitement, the courier first gave the report to the town recorder, who then aroused the mayor, who in turn made his way to the governor's mansion as day was breaking. Governor Floyd was horrified, but before he could mobilize the militia or send any guns he must have the approval of the Governor's Council—a "vain and foolish" ceremony required by the new state constitution. By the forms of that "wretched and abominable" document, Floyd groaned, "I must first require advice of council, and then disregard it if I please." When word came that all the councilmen were out of town, Floyd went into a tirade. What was he supposed to do, sit here on his haunches while the slaves butchered everybody in Virginia, all because of that accursed constitution? Finally, when one councilman—the lieutenant governor—showed up in Richmond, Floyd secured his rubber-stamp approval and dispatched express riders in all directions to alert the militia.

For a while, the governor and his advisors went through an anxious time: additional reports seemed to indicate that a general revolt had broken out, that Virginia and perhaps the entire South would soon be ablaze. But in all the suspense Floyd tried to be clear-headed and firm. He would hold all militia regiments north and west of Richmond in a state of readiness. He then ordered two Richmond outfits—an artillery unit and Captain Randolph Harri-

91

son's cavalry troop—to move at once to Southampton County. He also dispatched a total of two thousand guns there, sent word for the militia of Norfolk, Portsmouth, and Petersburg to march as well, and directed that Brigadier General Richard Eppes of Sussex County take charge of all military commands arriving in the stricken area.

Meanwhile Richmond was swirling with rumors, as worried citizens gathered on the commons and in the streets to find out the news. What was it? What had happened? Slave revolt down in Southampton, couriers said, worse than anything since Prosser and Santo Domingo, hundreds of Negroes murdering everybody in their path. "The intelligence has burst very unexpectedly upon us," reported the Richmond *Compiler*. "No one has had the slightest intimation or dream of such a movement." The paper added: "The wretches who have conceived this thing are mad—infatuated—deceived by some artful knaves, or stimulated by their own miscalculating passions."

In Richmond, passions ran high all Tuesday afternoon as cavalry and artillery clattered through the streets. Then word arrived that a huge slave army had been sighted moving out of the Dismal Swamp and heading this way. By late afternoon, volunteer units had set up barricades on the roads to Norfolk and Petersburg and armed patrols moved through the city, arresting unattended Negroes. Meanwhile, at the governor's mansion, the artillery and cavalry mustered and prepared to move with considerable fuss and fanfare. Among the horsemen was John Hampden Pleasants, twenty-four-year-old editor of the Richmond *Whig*. A graduate of William and Mary College and the son of a former Virginia governor, Pleasants was going along both as a soldier and as a sort of war correspondent for the *Whig*. As it turned out, he was the only genuine newspaperman to provide on-the-spot coverage from Southampton. Around 5 P.M. on Tuesday, Harrison's cavalry headed south with bugles blaring. The artillery was to depart by steamboat a few hours later.

At that the capital tightened its defenses and the governor and his advisors waited for news in a state of high tension. There were ugly reports of atrocities committed against blacks in and around Richmond, but Floyd and the newspapers emphatically denied that a reign of terror had broken out. Conceding that "we experience much anxiety here," the governor nevertheless insisted that Richmond was orderly on this dark and momentous day.

If Richmond was apprehensive, Portsmouth and Norfolk were transported with excitement. With bells tolling and volunteers clamoring in the streets, the mayor of Norfolk was beset with doomsday visions—of slave armies slashing their way to the coast, of white homes going up in flames. Convinced that the militia could not crush the rebellion alone, he prevailed on United States forces at Fortress Monroe for help. Soon several federal army and naval units were on their way to Southampton. And so were militia and vigilante outfits from neighboring Isle of Wight, Surry, and Sussex counties.[16]

Meanwhile news of the rebellion had spread into North Carolina and a number of communities there were also mobilizing. Choctaw Williams had ridden madly into Murfreesboro, some sixteen miles southeast of Cross Keys, and stunned people with what he'd seen at the Whitehead and Francis homesteads, crying that his own "wife & Deare little child" had been slaughtered with axes. Then Levi Waller arrived in town to corroborate the kind of atrocities Williams described. By now all was pandemonium in Murfreesboro. Would the insurgents invade North Carolina? Would the slaves here rise as well? Many of the town's militiamen were attending a revival over in Gates County, so that the place was almost defenseless. An old man was reported to have become so frightened he dropped dead of a heart attack. Women became "frantic with distress" when a messenger reported that a large body of Negroes was on Boon's Bridge and marching this way. It was a false alarm, but town authorities were taking no chances and sent a courier to retrieve the militiamen. After a killing ride, the man tore through the Gates County revival site, yelling that "the negroes have risen in Southampton and are killing every white person from the cradle up, and are coming this way." As the families raced away, the courier sped on to the Gates County Courthouse, where the local militia commander dispatched an official report to Governor Montford Stokes in Raleigh, requesting that arms and reinforcements be rushed to Gates and Hertford counties.

By Tuesday afternoon, the Governor's Guards had mustered in chaotic Murfreesboro and set out for Southampton, followed by other militia and vigilante groups. Soon over three thousand armed white men were on the march to Southampton from contiguous counties in North Carolina and Virginia, and hundreds more were mobilizing.[17]

Nat had barely gotten to sleep Monday night when a terrible racket woke him. He found his men thrashing about the woods in great disorder. A sentinel thought the militia was attacking from Ridley's house, and many of the slaves were panic-stricken. To reassure them, Nat sent a patrol out to reconnoiter, but when it returned most of the new recruits mistook it for the militia and deserted. By dawn on Tuesday only twenty insurgents were left.

In desperation they rode over to Dr. Simon Blunt's plantation, hoping to gain additional followers among his sixty-odd slaves. As the rebels paused at the gate, the place looked deserted in the gray light of morning. With Hark in the lead, they broke the gate down and moved cautiously up to the house and adjacent slave cabins. In a moment, Hark yelled and fired his gun to see if anybody was home.

Instantly gunshots exploded from the house, catching the insurgents completely by surprise. One white man boomed away from an upstairs window with a double-barrel shotgun, while another lay down a withering fire from the porch. They killed one Negro and wounded several others as their horses stampeded and carried them round and round the house. One volley knocked Hark to the ground, where he lay severely wounded. As Nat tried frantically to rally his men, Blunt's slaves charged out of the kitchen east of the house, yelling infernally and brandishing hoes, pitchforks, axes, and clubs. The slaves captured several insurgents and helped disperse the rest.

Later, when asked about the ambush and the loyalty of his slaves, Blunt explained it this way. A messenger had brought him news of the insurrection on Monday and had urged him to go down to Ridley's, where the militia was stationed. Well, the doctor was crippled—crippled with the gout—and decided to fight it out if the Negroes came his way. Joined by his overseer and three white neighbors,

Blunt and his son fortified the house and waited through the night. Meanwhile Blunt gathered his slaves around him and gave them the choice, he said, of standing with him or joining the rebels. They stood with him. Though Blunt did not say so, he surely added that the Negroes did not have a chance against the Virginia militia, that any of his slaves who joined the rebellion would either be shot or hanged.[18]

With most of his men shot or scattered, the Prophet crashed through the timber beyond Blunt's place, calling out for his lieutenants. At last Nat came across Will and a handful of other insurgents and led them back through the forests toward the Travis and Francis vicinity. The Prophet was distressed that Blunt's slaves had fought against him, but he still clung to the belief that somehow he could gather his scattered followers and mount another attack. At length the little party came to the Barrow Road, moving through the very neighborhood Nat's insurgent army had ransacked the previous morning. But the signs were ominous, for armed whites seemed everywhere—on the road, the forest paths. Darting through the trees, moving away from the yelling men and the dogs, the slaves came to Newit Harris's plantation, where Nat had exhorted his columns only yesterday and had sent them forward toward certain glory. But the slaves stopped at the edge of the woods, for armed men were prowling around the plantation house. *Militia.* In a moment they were pointing and running this way. The whites opened with a volley of musketry, and a brief, desperate skirmish flared in the forest. When it was over, three of Nat's men lay dead, their corpses left to rot under the trees. Among the dead was Will the executioner, Will the implacable axman, who wanted to gain his freedom or perish in the attempt. According to one writer, crows and vultures fed on the dead blacks until only their skeletons remained.

Skeletons and skulls, the Barrow Road, the crucifix and the sun. Little more than symbols were left. Somehow the Prophet and four others escaped from the militia and then stopped for a moment somewhere deep in the woods. Nat's men were terribly dejected—four human satellites, held to the Prophet by threads that were about to snap. Though shaken himself, Nat tried to exhort his followers, to resuscitate their fighting spirit. He ordered Curtis and Stephen Ridley to ride south and recruit in Newsom's and Allen's quarter. But they did not want to go. They had been drinking and anyway there was little left to fight for. Nat made them do as he said, contending that the whites were "too much alarmed to interrupt you."

So they set out southward on mules. They hadn't gone far when they came upon John Clark Turner, armed with a gun. The slaves insisted they were going home—they wasn't part of no ruction, no sir. But Turner was unimpressed, pointed out that they were heading in the opposite direction from Ridley's quarter. He stuck his gun in their backs and prodded them down to Cross Keys, where a number of other blacks had been imprisoned. Many white refugees were there, too, some of them survivors of the insurrection. Among them were Nathaniel and Lavinia Francis, who had located one another in the backwoods and come here for safety. The story goes that Nathaniel found two of his slaves among the Negro captives. One was Easter, a house servant who had protected Lavinia when Charlotte had attacked her with a knife. According to the story, Nathaniel hugged Easter and secured her release. Then he saw Charlotte. Seized by an uncontrollable rage, he dragged her outside, strapped her to an oak tree, and shot her to death.

After Curtis and Stephen had gone, Nat and the other two rebels made their way back to the Travis neighborhood and hid in the woods near the home place. It was now Tuesday night. All that remained of his insurgent force were the other Nat and a slave named Jacob. Still, the Prophet refused to give up, refused to believe that his faithful lieutenants had all been killed or captured. No, they must have gotten lost after the ambush at Blunt's plantation and were now looking for him in the forests somewhere. Rousing himself to one more burst of hope, he commanded Jacob and the other Nat to go out and find his scattered lieutenants. Tell them, the Prophet said, tell them to rally all the insurgents they can find and meet me again at Cabin Pond. Yes, then we will rise and fight again.

And now he was alone, a general without an army, a prophet without a follower, hiding in the swamps with only his prayers to give him comfort. By now, though, even his prayers had lost their magic. For whites were swarming through the countryside—proof that he had failed? proof that after just thirty-one hours his holy war had ended? proof that Jehovah for some inexplicable reason had deserted him? Nat made his way back to Cabin Pond and waited there all Tuesday night and Wednesday morning. A mile or so to the northwest was Giles Reese's place and Nat's own family . . . Cherry and his children. He could not go there, did not dare go there. On Wednesday afternoon, he spotted white patrols moving through the trees nearby. Had Jacob and Nat abandoned him too? Had they been captured and forced to betray his hideout? Where were his lieutenants, his signs, his visions and miracles . . . where are you, Hark? Where, Nelson? In deep anguish, Nat left Cabin Pond and shrank deep into the swamps. After dark, he stole back to the Travis farm, found it deserted, and helped himself to provisions. He could not return to the woods, crawling as they were with armed whites, so he ran out into the open, out across the meadows and cotton patches. On Thursday night, he came to a pile of fence rails in a field, dug a hole under the rails and crawled inside, intending "to lie by till better times arrive."[19]

All day Tuesday, August 23, Jerusalem was in a state of confusion and chaos. Hours after the skirmish at Harris's plantation, the militia officially mobilized and marched out of Jerusalem, ready to fight an insurgent army that no longer existed. On Wednesday General Eppes arrived with reinforcements and sent out patrols to find out what was happening. For the next forty-eight hours, United States troops, militiamen, and disorganized volunteers streamed into Jerusalem, adding to the uproar there.

Harrison's cavalry troop reached the town around nine o'clock Thursday morning, after "a rapid, hot and most fatiguing march." Pleasants reported to the *Whig* that the whole country was "thoroughly alarmed" and that Jerusalem itself was "crowded from its foundations." Some 250 federal troops were there, along with a large number of militia and some 400 hysterical women. Rumors flew that the slave army, estimated at 1,200 men, was still intact and that collateral rebellions had broken out in adjacent counties. Pleasants discounted such reports as wild exaggerations, but conceded that it was hard to distort the atrocities committed by the insurgents: "whole families, fathers, mothers, daughters, sons, sucking babes, and school children, butchered, thrown into heaps, and left to be devoured by hogs and dogs or to putrify on the spot." He estimated that from forty to one hundred slaves had actually been involved and contended that in spite of their ferocity, "twelve armed and resolute men were certainly competent to have quelled them at any time." Why had it taken Southampton so long to mobilize? Because, Pleasants said, whites there had been caught by surprise. Because they had thought first about sheltering their women and children and did not initially fight up to par. But by the time his outfit arrived, Pleasants observed, scouring parties were out and the insurrection was over.

But the killing was not. "Wound up to a high pitch of rage," whites mounted a full-scale manhunt in southeastern Virginia, prowling the woods and swamps in search of fugitive rebels and alleged collaborators. They chased the blacks down with howling dogs, shooting some on the run and dragging others back to jail in Jerusalem. One group of citizens decapitated Henry Porter and carried his head triumphantly through the county. Several insurgents fought back zealously, preferring to perish with guns in their hands than be taken by white men. Whites conceded that such slaves "died bravely, indicating no reluctance to lose their lives in such a cause." In the "agonies of their wounds," they announced that they were dying happily because "God had a hand in what had been done."

Among those who resisted were several free blacks—Billy Artis, Benjamin and Thomas Haithcock, and three boys. After the ambush at Blunt's plantation, they had ridden through the countryside in a frantic effort to raise slave allies. At one farm, with his slave wife at his side, Artis harangued some blacks, declaring that General Nat had fought the whites and had marched to Bellfield in Greensville County to kill whites there. Soon Nat would return, Artis exclaimed, and the Negroes must join him and fight like men. But with white patrols closing in on them, Artis and his companions realized that the end was near now, that the rebellion was dead. Yet they refused to give up. At another farm, Artis brandished a hatchet and told a slave that "he would cut his way, he would kill and cripple as he went." Later the free Negroes split up, everyone for himself. Eventually whites captured Thomas Haithcock and a couple of the others, but Artis chose to commit suicide rather than be executed or taken alive. The militia found him, dead, his hat hung on a stake nearby and a pistol at his side.

By Sunday, August 28, all the bona fide insurgents except Nat and five or six others had been killed or locked up in the small wooden jail in Jerusalem. The place was brimming with Negroes, some "very humble," whites reported, and "much grieved" at what had happened. Others, though, were reticent and inscrutable, swatting the flies away in their hot and rancid cells. There was Hark Travis, carried down from Blunt's plantation in bad shape from his wounds. There was Nelson Williams, captured by the militia near Cross Keys. There was Sam Edwards, found hiding under his master's house in the backwoods. There was hesitant Jack Reese, still wearing his master's shoes and socks, having given a "voluntary confession" to a white named Thomas C. Jones. There was Barry Newsom, Thomas Haithcock, Yellow Davy Waller, and young Moses Travis. The three teenage Francis boys were there, too, as were Jack and Andrew Whitehead, still as confused and distressed as they had been during the revolt itself.[20]

Some of the prisoners had surrendered voluntarily, for fear that furious whites might kill them. They had good reason to be afraid. For white vigilantes—and some militiamen—had gone on a rampage, shooting and axing every Negro they could find, women and children included. Some of these whites were boiling mad and wanted to avenge the atrocities they had found—"we saw several children whose brains had been kicked out," snapped one volunteer. But others joined in the carnage out of sheer racial hatred, having come to Southampton, as one man said, to "kill somebody else's niggers" without being held accountable for it. The story goes that a gang of horsemen set out from Richmond, vowing to kill every nigger in the stricken county. After a hard ride, they came upon a free black man hoeing in his field. "Is this Southampton County?" one asked. "Yes, Sir," the Negro replied, "you have just crossed the line, by yonder tree." The whites shot him dead.

The worst outrages were committed by a cavalry company from Murfreesboro. Divided into two detachments, the horsemen stormed through the Virginia backwoods, butchering some forty blacks in two days of unremitting violence. One column decapitated fifteen slaves and placed their heads on poles, where they remained for weeks "as a warning to all who should undertake a similar plot." The second detachment, after gunning down three blacks near the Whitehead place, divided up $23 found on one of the victims, "as they had as well be paid for the trouble as not."

And so the bloodletting went. At Cross Keys a mob lynched five luckless blacks. At the intersection of the Barrow Road and the Jerusalem highway, another vigilante outfit decapitated a Negro and mounted his head on a post (from then on the "grinning skull" was known as the Blackhead Sign Post). Down in North Carolina, distraught Murfreesboro residents shot and beheaded a slave accused of complicity in the Southampton revolt. In Enfield, the "good people about town" seized a free Negro, tried but failed to extort a confession from him, and shot him anyway. In all directions in upper North Carolina and southeastern Virginia, whites took Negroes from their shacks and tortured, shot, and burned them to death and then mutilated their corpses in ways that witnesses refused to describe. No one knows how many innocent Negroes perished in this reign of terror—at least 120, probably more. Several whites publicly regretted these atrocities but warned that they were the inevitable results of slave insurrection. Another revolt, they said, would end with the extermination of every black in the region.[21]

General Eppes, for his part, was so disturbed about white barbarities that on August 28 he issued a proclamation that any further outrages would be dealt with according to the articles of war. Since the insurrection was over, he asked the federal forces to leave, and except for a contingency force of fifty men, he ordered all volunteers and militia units to disband and go home as well. At the same time, the general scratched off a report to Governor Floyd that the rebellion had not been a concerted one and that no further hostilities were expected.

Eppes may have thought the danger had passed, but Southampton's residents had not. On August 29 a citizens' committee memorialized President Jackson about the insurrection: "so inhuman has been the butchery, so indiscriminate the carnage, that the tomahawk and scalping knife have now no horrors. . . . In the bosom of almost every family the enemy still exists." A Jerusalem resident wrote the Richmond *Enquirer* that "the oldest inhabitants of our county have never experienced such a distressing time, as we have had since Sunday night last." All over the county labor is paralyzed, whole farms and plantations are deserted, and "every house, room, and corner in this place is full of women and children, driven from home." "In almost every section of our county," another white recorded, "conversation instead of being as it was a month since, light and cheerful, is now cloathed in dismal forebodings.—Some of our citizens will leave us—and all agree, that they never again can feel safe, never again be happy."[22]

By now whites "down county" had identified Nat Turner as indisputably the leader of the revolt, and Southampton whites were asking the inevitable questions. Why had Nat rebelled? How could he commit such violence here, in mellow and enlightened Southampton County? How could their darkies be capable of such rage? such savagery? Equally inexplicable was what had happened to Nat. Was he hiding among somebody's slaves here in the county? Had he made his way into the Dismal Swamp, to organize another insurgent gang and strike again?

Before leaving for Richmond, John Hampden Pleasants tried to find out more about Nat Turner and the reasons for the insurrection. From whites who knew him, Pleasants learned that Nat was "a shrewd fellow" who "reads, writes, and preaches." He pretended to be a prophet and used religious tricks and connivances to gain control over his "ignorant" followers. But there was something about Nat that bothered Pleasants. If he was as smart as whites claimed, how could he believe an insurrection would end other than in disaster? Pleasants decided that religious fanaticism had clouded Nat's mind. "Being a fanatic, he possibly persuaded himself that heaven would intervene." Why, then, had he risen? Pleasants was inclined to think that Nat "acted upon no higher principle than the impulse of revenge against the whites, as the enslavers of him and his race," and the editor said so in a long account published later in the *Whig*.

Several Southampton men agreed with Pleasants about Nat's

fanaticism. Yes, the black mystic and holy man, whom whites had thought so harmless, was a religious maniac all right. And their opinion seemed confirmed when authorities located Nat's wife and lashed her until she surrendered Nat's papers—weird, sinister documents that passed into the possession of a Jerusalem lawyer, who seems to have been William C. Parker. In an unsigned letter to the *Whig,* the attorney wrote that some of these documents contained hieroglyphical characters, "conveying no definite meaning," while others had strange numerological calculations, "6,000, 30,000, 80,000 &c." On each paper were drawings of the crucifix and the sun, and the characters on the oldest document "appear to have been traced with blood." This was enough to send shivers down the strongest spines, and few whites who scrutinized Nat's papers could doubt his religious obsessions. But the documents revealed little about the revolt itself. One contained the names of some nineteen blacks—were these all that had been initially involved? Or had the uprising been part of a larger, more demonic plot against Virginia whites? The public demanded some answers, cried one Jerusalem resident, so that safeguards could be taken against similar outbreaks in the future.[23]

It was Wednesday, August 31. In a climate of profound disquiet, a Court of Oyer and Terminer convened in Jerusalem to try some forty-nine imprisoned Negroes on various charges of conspiracy, insurrection, and treason. There was to be no jury trial, though. A Court of Oyer and Terminer, which had jurisdiction over capital offenses among slaves, consisted of several justices who were appointed by the governor and his council and who themselves decided on the guilt or innocence of the accused. But excitement was so high in Jerusalem "that were the justices to pronounce a slave innocent," declared a group of responsible citizens, "we fear a mob would be the consequence." The court was worried, too, and persuaded Eppes to deploy an armed force about the jail to prevent a lynching. For the justices, all leading citizens of the county, the slave trials would demonstrate the integrity of their system, proving that in Virginia even mutinous slaves got a fair trial, that in all the heat and hysteria of the moment, the law would prevail in Southampton County.

Governor Floyd, too, was concerned about the trials. He understood only too well that his political future was at stake in how he dealt with them: he must prevent drumhead justice, but he must make certain that the guilty were punished. Accordingly Floyd sent explicit instructions to all county courts that planned to try suspected Negroes, directing that legal procedures be followed to the letter and that transcripts of all trials be authenticated by the sheriff and sent to him personally.

As the Jerusalem court came to order that Wednesday, the sheriff escorted eight slaves before the grim-faced judges, to be arraigned and tried. Observing all the judicial niceties, the court appointed a lawyer for each slave at a recompense of $10 per case. Three Jerusalem attorneys—William C. Parker, Thomas R. Gray, and James French—were to defend all the blacks tried in Jerusalem. Though Parker was a slaveholder himself and had commanded a party of volunteers during the rebellion, he was determined that the captured blacks should receive fair treatment. Nothing is known about French, but Gray was about sixty years old, had a childless wife around forty or so, and owned some seventeen slaves. All three men appear to have been liberal lawyers by Southern white standards, for they risked social ostracism in defending rebellious slaves—something not even the money they earned could entirely assuage.

As the trials progressed, it became evident that the most effective brake on summary justice was financial considerations. After all, the state of Virginia had to pay for all blacks consigned to the gallows, and if the judges resorted to mass hangings the cost would have been astronomical. But even so, the trials were hardly the picture of even-handed justice, for the judges convicted several blacks on highly questionable grounds. For example, the court found the three teenage Francis slaves guilty of conspiracy and insurrection, though all available evidence indicated that the insurgents had forced the boys along against their will and had guarded them with guns. Though the boys received death sentences, Floyd evidently commuted them to transportation outside the United States. Moreover, the judges convicted several slaves simply for talking rebellious, for saying they would help General Nat kill white folks if he came their way. One of the defense lawyers was dismayed about this and warned that if the court condemned blacks merely for belligerent remarks, there would be no end to the hanging.

Meanwhile angry crowds moiled in the street ouside—and once actually threatened to break into the jail and murder the slaves being held there. But Attorney Parker pleaded with the whites to give the Negroes a fair trial. To guard against lynch law on the one hand and further slave troubles on the other, Parker helped organize a company of Southampton volunteers and became their captain. They would wear dark gray uniforms trimmed with black braid and would drill until they were "No 1" in Virginia.

On Saturday, September 3, Sam, Hark, and Nelson all came to trial in a heavily guarded courthouse. Still suffering from his wounds, Hark had appeared in court once already, as a defense witness in Moses Barrow's trial. In it, Hark stated that Moses had joined the insurgents voluntarily and was with them at Blunt's plantation. Drawing on other slave testimony for the prosecution, the judges had found Moses guilty and sentenced him to hang. And now it was Hark's turn. Defended by William Parker, he pleaded not guilty to his charges, then watched in silence as prosecuting attorney Meriwether B. Broadnax summoned witnesses against him —first Levi Waller and then Thomas Ridley, who had interrogated Hark after his capture. To nobody's surprise, the judges found him guilty, sentenced him to death, and instructed the state to pay the Travis estate the sum of $450. By day's end, the court had also convicted Sam Francis, Nelson Williams, Yellow Davy Waller, and the other Nat, all of whom would hang with Hark on September 9.

On Saturday evening, Postmaster Thomas Trezevant summarized the progress of the trials in a letter to the Richmond *Whig*. Despite all the wild reports circulating in Virginia, Trezevant insisted that there was "no good testimony as yet to induce a belief that the conspiracy was a general one." The Southampton court had now tried fourteen Negroes and found thirteen guilty; thirty-five still awaited prosecution. The following day Trezevant added a postscript. "Sunday evening, 3 o'clock—Nothing more today. *We commence hanging tomorrow.*"[24]

As the trials went on in Southampton, whites across Virginia were still reeling with shock and disbelief. For Nat's rebellion was an eruption of black fury that rocked Virginia's white community to its foundations and sent concussions throughout all of Dixie. How, whites cried, could such racial violence happen in "civilized and virtuous" Virginia, where happy darkies and affectionate masters were supposed to love one another in idyllic harmony? And if it could happen in Virginia, what would stop the contagion from spreading across the "genteel" South from Wilmington to Charleston? In one desperate blow, Nat Turner had smashed the prevailing stereotype of master-slave relations in the Old South, forcing whites to confront a grim and dreaded reality—that all was not sweetness and sunshine in their slave world, that their own Nats and Harks might be capable of hatred and rebellion. And so whites stood face to face with their worst nightmares—their pretenses were gone for now— and from all directions there were voices of despair in the wind.

"We may shut our eyes and avert our faces, if we please," cried a South Carolinian when he heard the news, "but there it is, the dark and growing evil at our doors; and meet the question we must, at no distant day. . . . What is to be done? Oh! my God, I do not know, but something must be done."

"I view the condition of the Southern states as one of the most unenviable that can be conceived," lamented a North Carolina woman. "To be necessarily surrounded by those in whom we cannot permit ourselves to feel confidence, to know that unremitted vigilance is our only safeguard, & that sooner or later we or our descendants will become the certain victims of a band of lawless wretches, who will deem murder & outrage just retribution, is deplorable in the extreme. . . . Mr. L. regrets holding so much property here, & if not actually tied down to the place, would gladly remove to the North."

Declared a niece of George Washington: "It is like a smothered volcano—we know not when, or where, the flame will burst forth, but we know that death in the most horrid form threatens us. Some have died, others have become deranged from apprehension, since the South Hampton affair."[25]

Monstrous rumors fed on such fears. For weeks after the insurrection, reports of additional uprisings swept over the South, and scores of communities from Virginia to Mississippi convulsed in hysteria. In Alabama, frightened whites insisted that "the infection is pretty general with the negroes" and that bellicose Indians were plotting with them. In South Carolina, government and press alike tried to censor the news from Southampton, but word filtered down anyway, causing even greater consternation than the slave disturbances of the 1820s. Charleston was in such a panic about Nat Turner that the legislature approved a special cavalry force to protect the city. While no insurrections flared up in South Carolina, Governor James Hamilton suggested that the Southern states adopt joint measures to maintain internal security.[26]

The hysteria was worse in North Carolina, in the northeastern tier of counties along the Virginia border. The area crawled with rumors—of slave plots in Franklin County, of sinister movements on the big plantations along the Roanoke River. At Murfreesboro, where over a thousand refugees had gathered, armed men milled about in noisy confusion, and one reported that "tranquility cannot be soon restored." Another citizen wrote Governor Stokes that the militia should be deployed in every imperiled county, to march about with muskets loaded and swords drawn. North Carolina's slaves "must be convinced that they must and will be soon destroyed if their conduct makes it the least necessary."

In September, new alarms pummeled upper North Carolina. A man from Murfreesboro, having attended a slave trial in Virginia's Sussex County, reported back that the Southampton insurgents had expected armed slave resistance "from distant neighborhoods," including the large plantations on the Roanoke. Yes, the fellow cried, testimony in the Sussex trial "proved" that a concerted uprising was to have taken place in Virginia and upper North Carolina, where Negro preachers had been spreading disaffection, and that "dire and extensive would have been the slaughter but for a mistake in the day of commencement." The plan, the man said, called for the larger rebellion to begin on the last Sunday in August. But he contended that the Southampton rebels mistook August 21 as the target Sunday, all the while their North Carolina allies were waiting for August 28!

Though no such plan had existed, the report traumatized whites in the northeastern tier of counties, especially in neighborhoods with heavy slave concentrations. Couriers rode for Raleigh to beg for muskets and ammunition. Militia outfits mustered along the Roanoke, chased after imaginary insurgents, and shot, axed, imprisoned, and hanged still more innocent blacks. Phantom slave columns marched out of the Dismal Swamp, only to vanish when militia units rushed out to fight them.[27]

In mid-September came the most shattering alarm of all: couriers reported that a full-scale rebellion had blazed up in southeastern North Carolina, in Duplin and Sampson counties. Desperate messages claimed that slave insurgents had already massacred seventeen whites and were now attacking contiguous counties. Such communiqués were completely false, but frantic whites were now reacting to their own shadows. Militia commanders alerted their troops and sent off exaggerated reports to the governor, which gathered additional frills as express riders bore them to the capital. Meanwhile, mass hysteria gripped the town of Wilmington down near the Atlantic Ocean. Rumors flew that a slave army—maybe led by Nat Turner himself—had been seen moving out of Sampson and Duplin counties and was punching its way toward Wilmington. With church bells clanging, city officials declared martial law. Newspapers fanned the flames with sensational news of butchery and looting. Women and children locked themselves in churches and the bank. Armed horsemen clattered through the streets, and infantry units threw up barricades on the roads and byways.

But no slave army appeared. Out of blind vengeance, whites turned on the local Negro population and "by flogging and menaces" forced five hapless blacks into confessing that, yes, they were to meet insurgents from Sampson County and help murder all white men, women, and children in Wilmington. A court tried and convicted all five Negroes and had them shot and buried on Gallows Hill. For good measure, the court sent six additional blacks to the gallows; and a mob lynched four others as "a measure indispensable to the safety of the community."

Raleigh too was in turmoil, as a succession of express riders burst into the city with doomsday reports: slave rebels had allegedly set much of eastern North Carolina afire, had burned Wilmington, slaughtered half its population, and were moving "in large numbers" toward the capital itself, "murdering all before them" and committing "horrid butcheries." Raleigh newspapers added to the tumult by publishing these stories under lurid headlines. With whites swarming into town from outlying farms and plantations, Raleigh's militia dug in and the capital put itself "in a state of preparation for war."

In all the excitement, a few people managed to keep their heads. On September 16 the Raleigh *Star* corrected its initial reports and denied the disturbing news now "circulating through the country." A few days later the Raleigh *Register* admitted that its own account of insurrections in North Carolina had been "highly exaggerated." The storm had passed now, the paper declared, so that it was possible to ascertain the truth. While slaves in the southeastern part of the state had undoubtedly "talked about insurrection," none in fact had transpired.[28]

Over in the governor's mansion, Stokes sorted through all the high-decibel reports he'd received and reached the same verdict as the *Register*. "I have no doubt," he wrote Governor Hamilton of South Carolina, "but the news of the Virginia insurrection prompted the restless and unruly slaves, in a few instances to make a similar attempt in this State." Yet no "overt" rebellions had broken out anywhere in North Carolina, nor had anything like a concerted plot actually been uncovered. Stokes conceded that unbridled terror had seized whites in the eastern black belt and that "among the negroes condemned and executed, some, who were innocent, have suffered." Nevertheless, the governor considered the danger far from over. Later he advised the legislature that it was impossible to conceal from the world, and "needless to disguise from ourselves," the fact that the slaves had become increasingly discontented and ungovernable. He blamed Negro unrest on "fanatics of their own complexion and other incendiaries" and insisted that North Carolina strengthen its military forces, so as "to guard against these evils, which in all probability will continue. . . ."[29]

If North Carolina was contending against phantom insurrectionaries, so was embattled Virginia. Even after General Eppes announced that Nat's rebellion had ended, accounts of collateral uprisings and pleas for help swept into Richmond from every direction—from Northampton, Amherst, Prince Edward, Westmoreland, Prince George, and King and Queen counties, from Leesburg, Danville, Petersburg, Fredericksburg, Culpeper Courthouse, and dozens of other communities. All across the state whites formed patrols and vigilance committees, seized suspicious Negroes, fired off shotguns, and clamored for muskets from Richmond. In Charlottesville, students at the University of Virginia organized a volunteer outfit and prepared to engage any insurgents who came their way. In Bowling Green, whites insisted that their slaves had known about Nat Turner *before* he rebelled, and that black preachers would lead a mass revolt here on October 1. At Madison Courthouse an artillery company of "picked and chosen men" was ready "for any alarming circumstances." Rumors shook Stafford County that slaves in the stone quarries had risen. From Chesterfield came anguished cries for protection against "an enemy that is restless in their disposition and savage in their nature." Never had Virginians been so frightened. "These insurrections have alarmed my wife so as really to endanger her health," said one man, "and I have not slept without anxiety in three months. Our nights are sometimes spent in listening to noises. A corn song, or a hog call, has often been the subject of nervous terror, and a cat, in the dining room, will banish sleep for the night. There has been and there still is a *panic* in all the country."

Richmond too was jittery and full of foreboding, as express riders sped in and out of the city and wagons loaded with muskets, pistols, and swords rumbled away to infected neighborhoods. At the governor's mansion, Floyd and his advisors waded through all the reports of slave disturbances and demands for guns—was Virginia about to be consumed in a racial holocaust?—and cursed the day the militia's weapons had ever been removed to centrally located armories like that in Richmond. With Virginia in chaos, Floyd did all he could to meet the crisis, dispatching arms to distressed communities, sending additional weapons to counties with the heaviest slave populations, keeping the militia on the alert (especially near the coal mines and stone pits where slaves seemed conspicuously rebellious), and advising militia commanders to employ shotguns and bayonets freely against Negro insurgents.[30]

But the more embellished communiqués the governor received, the more dubious he became about all the "rumors and surmises" about Virginia's slaves. After all, General Eppes insisted that hostilities had been confined to Southampton and that no widespread plot had been uncovered. And in early September, in the pages of the Richmond *Whig,* John Hampden Pleasants impugned the "false, absurd, and idle rumors" which the Turner revolt had generated and contended that "the truth will turn out to be that the conspiracy was confined to Southampton, and that the idea of its extensiveness originated in the panic which seized upon the South East of Virginia."[31] So that Floyd himself could form "a just opinion" about the extent of the danger, he instructed militia commanders to furnish proof that slaves had risen in their districts. At the same time, the governor began receiving transcripts of the trials under way in Southampton and several adjacent counties and he pored over these, too, both to commute death sentences (when the court advised it) and to find any evidence of a widescale design. By September 10 Floyd concluded that no further revolts were likely and he wrote Eppes and other militia commanders so. A few days later he confided in his diary that "the slaves are quiet and evince no disposition to rebel," even though he was still receiving almost daily alarms, especially from the Blue Ridge Mountains, and was still sending weapons to the more disturbed communities.

The governor did his best to convince people that "there is no danger," that the slaves "were never more humble and subdued," and that in actual fact no additional insurrections had taken place in Virginia. Thanks to Floyd, Pleasants, and other level-headed men, the hysteria over Nat Turner eventually subsided. But all the work and tension left the governor feeling sickly. He was feverish and thirsty and had a bad taste in his mouth. He did not think his health could ever be restored in Richmond's damp climate. He longed for his home in Montgomery County in the Appalachians— longed for "my own mountain air" and the peace and tranquility there.

Though the Southampton nightmare seemed at an end, the governor was extremely irritated at what had happened to his state. What really irked him—even more than the false alarms—was the behavior of those "cowards" at Norfolk. Besides losing their reason like almost everybody else, the spineless mayor and his timid advisors had begged federal forces at Fortress Monroe to help suppress the Southampton insurrection. In Floyd's mind this was unforgivable, and he said as much in letters to the mayor and to a U.S. artillery commander in Norfolk. Did the mayor not understand that his actions could have resulted in calamity had the revolt been general? Since the governor had sent the Norfolk and Portsmouth militia to Southampton, the departure of United States forces— thanks to the mayor's "alarm" and lack of "reflection"—had left the Norfolk region virtually unguarded. Had the slaves risen there, it could have led to "a serious evil," inasmuch as the James River area had a large Negro population and a disparity in force. Well, *Floyd* had thought about all this; that is why he had *not* called on United States troops for assistance. He knew they would be needed in eastern Virginia in case of a mass uprising. But there was more to it than that. State rights and state pride were also involved. The governor wanted Virginians to crush the insurrection by themselves, without any help from Andrew Jackson's federal army. Floyd did not want the national government to do for Virginia what the state could do and must do for itself. Moreover, if the Negroes realized that Virginia had to rely on the national army for defense, would they not conclude that the Old Dominion could not fight its own battles? Well, the governor said, "it is not difficult to perceive the train of thought which would be indulged, should the United States at any future day have to use their forces in the prosecution of a foreign war."

As the governor fussed about Norfolk and "the cowardly fears of that town," he worried too about the impact of Nat's rebellion on Virginia's commercial credit. It was something he considered "not all pleasant." For if the insurrection destroyed Virginia's credit rating, how could she borrow enough money to subsidize the internal improvements Floyd envisioned? And while he brooded about that, he griped about the state constitution, too, which required advice of council for all important executive actions. It was like trying to work with his hands tied. For example, on September 27, the governor received from Southampton the trial records of three condemned slaves. The court recommended mercy for one, but Floyd could not grant it without consent of council—and once again not a single councilman was in town. So the "poor wretch" must lose his life—all because of that abominable constitution.

There were a great many abominations that blustery September. As Floyd scrutinized trial records from southeastern Virginia and rummaged through stacks of reports and communiqués, he decided quite emphatically that the Nat Turner outbreak was not the work of a solitary fanatic. *Of course* Virginia's slaves were quiet now. *Of course* there had been no mass revolt. That did not preclude the existence of a conspiracy behind the Southampton inferno, and the governor had a growing suspicion that one did exist. And he kept a special folder, marked *"Free Negroes & Slaves,"* in which he filed away all the evidence he could locate to prove his suppositions. In the folder were letters from Virginia postmasters, private citizens, and militia commanders who blamed all slave disturbances on the Quakers, Yankee vendors, Yankee evangelists, Yankee abolitionists, free Negroes, and black preachers—especially black preachers. "The whole of that massacre in Southampton is the work of these preachers," Floyd told his diary, and decided that they and all their slave congregations must be suppressed.[32]

While the governor collected information about the insurrection, Jerusalem whites had not been idle. Defense lawyers Parker and Gray had learned something about the revolt from the trials, though much remained unexplained about the motives and objectives of Nat Turner himself. Moreover, certain Jerusalem men—probably Parker and Gray and Postmaster Trezevant—had written unsigned accounts of the uprising for several newspapers. Most of these letters to the editor reflected a growing white consensus that Nat Turner was indeed a religious fanatic, his mind transported beyond all reason by a maniacal religious obsession.

Of the letters, the most illuminating was dated Jerusalem, September 17, and appeared in the Richmond *Whig* a few days later. Internal evidence strongly suggests that William C. Parker was the author. Drawing on evidence gathered from the slave trials and from interviews with blacks and whites alike, the author contended that unbridled religious revivalism had created a combustible atmosphere which ignited the Turner explosion. While he singled out Negro preachers for special censure, the author blamed white evangelists, too, who punctuated their sermons with a "ranting cant about equality" and who invited black exhorters to retail that doctrine to their congregations. The author insisted that such frenzied religious activities be sharply curtailed lest they cause another slave revolt. As for Nat himself, the author denied that he had ever preached (the author was wrong), arguing that Nat had merely exhorted and sung at Negro meetings. But the author observed that in his immediate neighborhood Nat had acquired "the character of a Prophet" and so his rebellion was indeed "the work of fanaticism"—"to an imagination like Nat's, a mind satisfied of the possibility, of freeing himself and race from bondage; and this by supernatural means." Still, the author noted that a huge majority of Southampton's slaves refused to enlist in Nat's crusade and he praised them for their forbearance. If Nat's grisly deeds repelled the author, so did the butchery of innocent Negroes, and he roundly condemned whites who had perpetrated these atrocities. "Should not the violated laws of their country call them to a settlement? They must bear in mind that the matter has one day to be adjudicated before an impartial judge." Echoing Eppes, Pleasants, and other Jerusalem letter writers, the author insisted that Nat's rebellion was not the product of a wide slave conspiracy. Yet, the author lamented, "scarcely a mail arrives that does not bring some account of an isolated conviction for insurrection in remote counties —thus Spottsylvania, Nansemond, Prince George, &c. Should the views here taken by me, prove that the insurrection was not a general one, and therefore save the life of a human being, I shall be more than compensated for the time consumed, together with the odium called down upon me, by the expression of my opinion." This clearly sounds like William Parker, who had implored whites in Jerusalem to give the slaves a fair trial, helped organize a volunteer company to maintain order there, and risked public odium by defending "niggers" in a court of law. What, then, should whites do to prevent another slave revolt? "The excitement having now subsided, which induced many to think wrong, and prevented many who thought right from stemming the tide, it becomes us as men to return to our duty. Without manifesting a fear of the blacks, by keeping a stationed armed force in any section of our country let us adopt a more efficient plan, by keeping up for some time a regular patrol, always under the command of a discreet person, who will not by indiscriminate punishment, goad these miserable wretches into a state of desperation."[33]

Meanwhile "the great banditti chief," as newspapers called Nat, was still at large. Parker and other Jerusalem residents thought he had left the state, but Governor Floyd was not so sure. On September 13 he decided to offer a reward for Nat's capture and wrote Eppes for a description. The governor's request fell into the hands of William C. Parker, who set about interviewing "persons acquainted with Nat from his infancy." Parker returned a portrait forthwith. "He is between 30 & 35 years old—five feet six or 8 inches high—weighs between 150 & 160 rather bright complexion but not a mulatto—broad-shouldered—large flat nose—large eyes—broad flat feet rather knock kneed—walk brisk and active—hair on the top of the head very thin—no beard except on the upper lip and tip of the chin. A scar on one of his temples produced by the kick of a mule—also one on the back of his neck by a bite—a large knot on one of the bones of his right arm near the wrist produced by a blow."

On September 17 Floyd issued an official proclamation of reward for Nat's capture, quoting Parker's description on the reverse side. The proclamation offered $500 to anybody who conveyed Nat to the Southampton County jail, and enjoined "the good people of the Commonwealth" to exert all their energies in finding the fugitive, "that he may be dealt with as the law directs." The proclamation appeared in the press and went out to Virginia postmasters, who tacked it up on doors and tree trunks for whites and blacks alike to see. All told, there was now $1,100 in various rewards offered for Nat's capture.

By late September a vast dragnet was out for the Prophet, but the man had apparently vanished. Predictably, rumors multiplied that Nat had been found drowned in western Virginia, that he'd been seized in Washington, D.C., that he'd escaped to the West Indies, that he'd been chased "armed to the teeth" into the mud and weeds along the Nottoway River. One report placed him 180 miles west of Southampton, near Fincastle in Botetourt County. "Stop him!" shrieked a Fincastle newspaper. And stories spread through town that Nat had been seen on the open road with a hymn book, believed to be on his way to Ohio.[34]

The truth was that Nat had never left Southampton County. For six weeks, he hid in his dugout under the fence rails, in a field not far from Cabin Pond. Initially he left the cave only for a few moments at night, to fetch water from a pond nearby. During the days, aroused whites prowled the traces and woods around him, and Nat lay in his hole scarcely daring to move. But in a few days hunger began to gnaw in him, and he took to venturing out at night to pilfer food from neighboring farms. Occasionally he eavesdropped at some farmhouse, crouched in the shadows below a window, hoping to hear something about Hark, Nelson, and the rest. One night he crept up to Nathaniel Francis's home—a desperate face at the windowpanes. Perhaps he saw lanterns flickering inside, heard Nathaniel and Lavinia, large now with child, talking in the living room around the fireplace. Behind Nat were the slave cabins, but he did not dare go there, for fear that some of the slaves might panic and give him away. An outsider, hunted by a host of armed whites, feeling forsaken by his God and his people, Nat ran away in the night, going to another farm, and another, until at last he returned in despair to his hideout. Never had he felt more alone. As the days passed, autumn leaves swirled against the fence rails. Shivering in his hole, Nat could hear slaves singing in the distance— it was cotton-picking time. October 2 was his birthday. He was thirty-one years old.

One night he wandered through the woods until dawn. Should he leave the county? stay? fight the whites until they killed him? Coming back to his hideout, he saw something move there. A slave? A militiaman? It turned out to be a dog, attracted to some meat Nat had stored away. He chased the animal off.

But a few nights later, as Nat was leaving for another nocturnal walk, the dog returned with a couple of Negroes, who were out hunting. The dog spotted the Prophet and yapped and snarled at him. When he approached, the two Negroes were stunned—could this tattered and dismal creature be Preacher Nat? The Prophet begged them not to betray him, begged them to keep his whereabouts a secret. But they fled, frightened to their bones.

Nat knew they would tell the whites—and they did. The news spread across the county like a timber fire—the "nigger" was here, right here in Southampton! Within twenty-four hours scores of whites swarmed through the countryside, all hoping to catch Nat and collect those rewards.

In all the tumult, Nat abandoned his hideout and ran through the woods and swamps, pursued "almost incessantly." Twice, three times, he tried to leave Southampton, but the county was cordoned off with horseback patrols. Hiding by day and moving by night, he circled Cabin Pond like a human satellite, with bloodhounds yowling in the distance. By now he was so desolate that he thought about surrendering. Why run any more? What was the use? Once he got within two miles of Jerusalem, only to change his mind and return to the Travis neighborhood. For several days he hid at some of the very farms his insurgents had attacked back in August. At last he came back to the Francis place and concealed himself in a fodder stack in a field. He could not run any longer. Hungry and hopeless, he decided to give himself up to Nathaniel Francis. He'd known Nathaniel all his life, had played with him when they were boys, had called him Nathaniel without the "Mr." and lived with his sister for nine years. Surely Nathaniel would not torture him, but would treat him like a prisoner of war.

On October 27 or 28, Nathaniel came riding by to inspect his fodder stacks. He was armed with a shotgun. To his astonishment, Nat—at least it looked like Nat—stepped out from one of the stacks. He was smiling. He was also carrying a sword. At once Nathaniel opened fire, and Nat staggered back with his hat blown off his head. Miraculously, he was not hurt, but Francis was loading up again, so Nat grabbed his hat and ran for his life.

Within the hour some fifty whites were in pursuit, but the Prophet eluded them, moving away from the fields in a zigzag course. At length, two miles northwest of Francis's farm, he dug another cave under the top of a fallen tree and scrambled inside. Around noon on Sunday, October 30, a patrol crashed through the forest where Nat was hiding. After the whites had gone, the Prophet tried to improve his camouflage, rearranging the brush and tree limbs. Then he stuck his head out to have a look around . . . *no!* There stood a white man, aiming a shotgun straight at him. As in a dream, the man ordered Nat to give up or get his brains blown out. Since the shotgun was "well charged," Nat had no choice but to throw down his sword. And so his odyssey ended as it had begun, on Sunday—the Lord's Sabbath—a mile and a half from the Travis house.

Nat's captor turned out to be one Benjamin Phipps, a poor

farmer who lived nearby and who'd come through the woods on his way to a neighbor's place, only to stumble on Nat quite by accident. There Phipps was, resting under a tree before continuing his journey, when who should pop out of a fallen tree—pop right out of the ground itself—but the most wanted "nigger" in all Virginia, with over a thousand dollars on his head. After Phipps had captured Nat and tied his hands, the white man fired his shotgun in the air and yelled in ecstasy. At last his neighbors came up and helped him shove the Prophet through the woods to Peter Edwards's plantation. There was a great clamor in the yard as whites and slaves alike crowded around the insurgent leader. They could only have been shocked at what they saw, for Nat was ragged and emaciated, "a mere scarecrow."[35]

Yet he held his head high. No matter how forlorn he had been as a fugitive, he now faced his enemies with a fierce pride. Soon a hundred people had congregated at the Edwards place, the men whooping and firing their guns overhead, the women inching up, like moths drawn to fire, to get a closer look at the notorious black prophet. By now riders were on their way to Jerusalem with the joyous news, and throughout the backwoods church bells were tolling. From Jerusalem couriers would carry the news up to Petersburg and Richmond, a happy Governor Floyd would issue an official proclamation, and newspapers all over the South would soon be blazing, "THE BANDIT TAKEN," "NAT TURNER SURELY IS CAPTURED."

Meanwhile a retinue of armed whites marched Nat down to Cross Keys, exhibiting him at farms and plantations along the way. But the crowds became increasingly menacing, as jubilation gave way to resentment and hatred. Lynch-mob voices cried for Nat's head. Men shook their fists and women screamed at him; boys ran up, spit in his face, ran off. Perhaps to appease their furious neighbors, Nat's guards gave him a public whipping. Through it all Nat "just grinned," a white man reported, and refused to repent. To save his life, the guards barricaded him in a farmhouse for the night.

The next day—Monday, October 31—Nat and his escort set out on the road to Jerusalem, on a slow, cold journey through a sea of hostile whites. At last, at 1:15 that afternoon, Nat marched across the main bridge into Jerusalem, still holding his head up, still wearing his shell-torn hat. Again, a mob thronged the streets as Nat struggled by. A visitor from Petersburg thought Jerusalem whites showed remarkable forbearance in not lynching "the wretch" on the spot. An extra guard muscled through the crowds and somehow got Nat inside the courthouse without injury.[36]

Nat now stood before a couple of court justices—James Trezevant and James W. Parker—who desired to question the prisoner without pressure or promises. Nat confronted the judges and said he was ready and willing to talk. As the interrogation began, to last about two hours, all the whites in the courtroom listened intently, hoping to find out more about this mysterious and prodigious black man who had so profoundly altered their lives. Among the observers were Postmaster Trezevant, taking notes for the Norfolk *American Beacon,* and two other Jerusalem men who would write unsigned communiqués for the Richmond *Enquirer* and the Richmond *Whig.* All three correspondents thought Nat "a shrewd, intelligent fellow" and the writer for the *Enquirer* was especially impressed with the Prophet's eyes: "They are very long, deeply seated in his head and have rather a sinister expression."

As the interrogation progressed, Nat spoke with unflinching candor. He stated emphatically that *he* had instigated and directed the slaughter of all those white people, though he had killed only Margaret Whitehead. He declared that the idea of insurrection had been evolving in his mind for several years, and he went on to recount the signs he'd seen in the heavens, the miracles and revelations the Spirit had shown him. He warned the judges that "I am in particular favor with heaven," insisting that God had given him extraordinary powers over the weather and the seasons, that "by the efficacy of prayer" he could cause raging thunderstorms or searing droughts. In addition, he could heal disease "by the imposition of his hands." In fact, he had once cured a comrade "in that manner."

Nat then described "the signed omens" by which Jehovah had commanded him to undertake his mission of death against the whites. In response to questions about the extent of the conspiracy, the Prophet denied that anybody besides himself and five or six others had known about his plot. His original target date was July

4, 1831, but he admitted that he "dreaded to commence." Then came the day of the black sun, which convinced him that God wanted him to move. He then imparted his plan to his closest lieutenants, "all of whom seemed prepared with ready minds and hands to engage in it." In shocking detail, he told how they assassinated the Travis family with axes. Initially they resorted to "indiscriminate massacre" in order to strike terror and alarm, but had they gained a foothold, Nat explained, "women and children would afterwards have been spared, and men too who ceased to resist."

During the interrogation, the *Enquirer* correspondent pressed Nat as to precisely how his so-called "signs" had figured in the insurrection, but Nat seemed vague about this, the correspondent said, and tended to "mystify" everything. When asked whether he'd done wrong in committing insurrection, Nat shook his head without hesitation. No, he had not done wrong. Even though he'd failed, even though he may have been deceived, he believed even now that he was right. And if he could do it all over again, he asserted, "he must necessarily act in the same way."

The whites listened to all this with mixed emotions. While Justice James Trezevant considered Nat's presentation "a medley of incoherent and confused opinions about his communication with God," Postmaster Trezevant thought Nat answered "every question clearly and distinctly, and without confusion or prevarication." They all agreed, however, that Nat labored under "as perfect a state of fanatical delusion as ever wretched man suffered."

After the interrogation, Postmaster Trezevant hurried off to prepare his account for the *American Beacon*. In it, he contended that Nat acknowledged himself "a coward," admitted that he had "done wrong," and advised all other Negroes "not to follow his example." Nat, of course, had said nothing of the kind. Trezevant was resorting to sheer propaganda, both to reassure white readers and to discourage any blacks who might see the postmaster's report.

For his part, the *Enquirer* correspondent wanted more facts about Nat Turner and his insurrection, because he believed all Virginia was anxious to know exactly why and how the thing had happened. And in his report to the *Enquirer*, the man admitted that he had hoped to provide "a detailed confession," but he understood that another gentleman was to record one "verbatim from Nat's own lips, with a view of gratifying public curiosity; I will not therefore forestall him." The gentleman mentioned was defense attorney Thomas R. Gray.

With Nat's trial set for November 5, armed guards conveyed him through the turbulent streets and locked him up in the condemned hole of the county jail. Here Nat found several of his free black followers—among them Barry Newsom and Thomas Haithcock —all bound over to the Superior Court for trial. From them Nat finally learned what had happened to his lieutenants. Hark, Nelson, and Sam had been hanged. Henry had been beheaded at or near Cross Keys. Hesitant Jack Reese had been sentenced to hang, but evidently the governor had commuted the sentence to transportation. Several others had also been hanged, including the other Nat, Yellow Davy Waller, Dred Francis, and Moses and Lucy Barrow. Convicted for trying to "detain" Mary Barrow, Lucy was the only female executed for the insurrection.

After the jailor had secured Nat with manacles and chains, to make certain he could not escape, a white man asked what had happened to all the money Nat had stolen from butchered whites. Nat retorted that he had taken exactly 75 cents. Then he turned to one of the free Negroes. "You know money was not my object."[37]

Sometime on Tuesday, November 1, the jailor unlocked Nat's cell and an elderly white man entered with paper and pen. It was cold and musty in the condemned hole, where Nat lay on a pine board "clothed in rags and covered with chains." Nat recognized the man as Thomas Gray, knew he had defended some of the other insurgents. Gray and the jailor were chums, so that the attorney had ready access to the prisoners. Gray assured Nat that neither the sheriff nor the court had sent him, that he was acting entirely on his own. Like Parker and several other Jerusalem men, who may in fact have cooperated with him, Gray thought that public curiosity was "much on the stretch" to know the reason for the insurrection. For Southampton whites simply could not fathom why their slaves would revolt, why they would perpetrate such a "fiendish" and "atrocious" slaughter. In Gray's opinion, the slave trials thus far had revealed little satisfactory evidence about motives and objectives. In truth, the entire affair was still "wrapt in mystery." So what Gray wanted from Nat was this: he wanted to take down and publish a full confession that would tell the public the facts about the insurrection, thus setting to rest all the "thousand idle, exaggerated and mischievous reports" that had rocked Virginia and all the rest of Dixie. What Gray had in mind were the wild rumors about concerted revolts in Virginia and North Carolina—rumors that had resulted in the deaths of many innocent Negroes. And many more were apt to perish unless Nat gave a statement about the exact nature and extent of the insurrection.

Evidently Nat trusted Gray and said he was willing to talk. And why shouldn't he? Though Nat never said so, this would be his last opportunity to strike back at the slave world he hated, to flay it with verbal brilliance and religious prophecy (was not exhortation his forte?). Indeed, a published confession would ensure Nat a kind of immortality; it would recount his extraordinary life in his own words and on his own terms; it would explain to posterity how he, the Negro slave called Nat Turner, had been the sole contriver of what Gray called "the first instance in our history of an open rebellion of the slaves," one so destructive it had shaken Southerners everywhere. Clearly a man with Nat's sense of destiny would not pass up a chance like this, so, yes, he would give the man a confession.

With Gray writing as rapidly as he could, Nat began. "SIR, You have asked me to give a history of the motives which induced me to undertake the late insurrection, as you call it—To do so I must go back to the days of my infancy, and even before I was born. . . ." Nat described his precociousness on Benjamin Turner's place—his powers of recollection, the ease with which he learned to read and write, the eminence he attained among slaves and whites alike. He told how his family, his master, and white men of the gospel had praised him for his brilliance and hinted that he was too intelligent to remain a slave . . . how the Spirit had spoken to him . . . and how in man's estate he had become a leader of his people and a prophet of Almighty God, ordained for a special destiny. He related carefully now how his visions, miracles, and revelations had led him to rebellion . . . how God had thundered in the heavens and announced to him that "the Serpent was loosened, and Christ had laid down the yoke he had borne for the sins of men, and that I should take it on and fight against the Serpent, for the time was fast approaching when the first should be last and the last should be first."

"Do you not find yourself mistaken now?" Gray interrupted.

Nat replied testily, "Was not Christ crucified?"

He explained that by signs in the heavens God had commanded him to rise "and slay my enemies with their own weapons." Then he embarked on a graphic, chilling account of the entire insurrection that was bound to awe readers for generations to come. As he had done in court on Monday, Nat insisted that the revolt was local in origin. When Gray questioned him about the reported uprising in North Carolina at about the same time, Nat denied any knowledge of it. But he warned that other slaves could well have seen visions and signs in the skies and acted as he had done. By the end of the confession, Nat was in high spirits, fiercely unrepentant and entirely "willing to suffer the fate that awaits me."

Nat talked for two days. On the third day Gray put him through a rigorous cross-examination and found his statement truthful and sincere, "corroborated by every circumstance coming within my own knowledge or the confessions of others whom had been either killed or executed."

Frankly Gray was impressed with this Negro man "whose name has resounded throughout our widely extended empire." If Nat was under ordinary height, he was nevertheless "strong and active, having the true negro face, every feature of which is strongly marked." Though Gray also judged Nat "a complete fanatic," he emphatically denied that Nat was ignorant or a coward. On the contrary, in native intelligence and quickness of perception Nat was surpassed by few men Gray had ever seen. And Nat could be intimidating. When, in a burst of enthusiasm, he spoke of the killings and raised his manacled hands toward heaven, "I looked on him," Gray said, "and my blood curdled in my veins."[38]

Since then, some critics have questioned the authenticity of the confessions to Gray, inasmuch as the latter was a white slaveholder and whatever Nat said was obviously filtered through his senses. Others have disparaged the document because Gray's motives seem suspect: here was a chance to get a dramatic story that would become a best seller and make Gray a lot of money. So how can it be the truth? Other critics have accused Gray of inventing a white myth about Nat as a ghoulish maniac, driven to insurrection by his religious phobias and fixations, and so a freak, an aberration whose likes would never appear in the South again. To these critics, then, the confession is unalloyed white propaganda, fabricated by Gray to ease Southern fears.[39]

When the document is viewed in historical context, these arguments seem unfair. The fact is that the confessions are very close to what Nat had already said in his October 31 court interrogation. And most details in the statement, as Gray said, can be corroborated by the slave trial records and by contemporary newspaper accounts, including the unsigned letters from Jerusalem (publishing anonymous communiqués was a common practice in those days). In the published *Confessions*, which appeared later in 1831, some remarks attributed to Nat were clearly Gray's—such as the assertions that whites arrived at Parker's cornfield in time "to arrest the progress of these barbarous villains" and that "we found no more victims to gratify our thirst for blood." But in most particulars—especially those on Nat's background, religious visions, and the revolt itself—the confessions seem an authentic and reliable document.[40]

In significant ways, instead of assuaging white fears, the confessions could only have heightened them. Gray did not censor Nat's description of his own intelligence or of the black rage that attended the killings. If Postmaster Trezevant, for the benefit of his readers, belittled Nat as an apologetic coward, Gray did not mince his words about Nat's courage, ferocity, and single-mindedness.

When Gray called Nat "a gloomy fanatic," he was merely repeating what Parker, Pleasants, and many other whites had long since decided. Like them, Gray had to believe that the insurrection sprang from religious fanaticism, which had bewildered and deranged Nat's mind and had led him and his "band of savages" to commit atrocities beyond the capacity of ordinary slaves. Whites like Gray could not blame the rebellion on their own slave system— they were too much a part of it to do that. And anyway, in their view Nat *was* a fanatic. In recounting his heavenly visions and in describing how God had called him to revolt, Nat was inviting skeptical whites to draw their own conclusions.

On November 5, the day of Nat's trial, a large and boisterous crowd gathered in Jerusalem. Fearing that Nat might be lynched, the sheriff recruited additional deputies to escort the Prophet from the jail over to the courthouse. As the deputies guarded the doors, Nat's trial opened, with Meriwether B. Broadnax as prosecuting attorney and Jeremiah Cobb as the presiding judge. An eminent citizen of the county, Cobb had a large family and possessed an impressive home and some thirty-two slaves. Present with Cobb were James Trezevant, James W. Parker, and several other justices.

Pounding his gavel, Cobb brought the court officially to order, appointed William C. Parker as Nat's counsel, and had the clerk read the charges. "Nat alias Nat Turner a negro man slave the property of Putnam Moore an infant" is "charged with conspiring to rebel and making insurrection."

Levi Waller was the first witness for the prosecution. Waller testified that he saw the insurgents murder several members of his family. Nat, whom Waller "knew very well," was clearly in command and forced the more reluctant rebels to mount up and ride with him. Trezevant next took the witness stand and repeated what Nat had said in his interrogation on October 31. Trezevant added, referring to the confessions Nat had given to Gray, that the accused had furnished "a long account of the motives which led him finally to commence the bloody scene." Thereupon the clerk read the confessions before the court, and Nat "acknowledged the same to be full, free and voluntary."

Parker had no witnesses or evidence to introduce in Nat's behalf—his conviction was a foregone conclusion—and the attorney submitted his case without argument. Nat, however, pleaded not guilty because he did not feel so. Judge Cobb, speaking for a unanimous court, pronounced Nat guilty as charged and asked if he had anything to say before sentencing. "Nothing but what I've said before," Nat replied.

It was therefore the order of the court, Cobb intoned, that Nat be returned to jail, where he was to remain until Friday, November 11, when, between the hours of ten in the forenoon and four in the afternoon, the sheriff was to escort the prisoner to the usual place of execution and hang him by the neck until he was dead. The judge then valued Nat at $375, which the state was to pay the Putnam Moore estate. With that, Cobb pounded his gavel and the court proceeded to another trial unrelated to the insurrection.

Around noon on November 11, the sheriff took Nat out to a field just northeast of Jerusalem and led him to a gnarled old tree which served as Southampton's gallows. Since a public hanging was a form of entertainment in those days, an immense crowd had gathered in the field to witness the spectacle. The sheriff gestured at the people and agreed to let Nat say something if he wanted. But Nat rejected the offer. "I'm ready," he told the man in a firm voice. As the sheriff placed the noose about his neck, Nat waited under the tree in composed and resolute silence, staring out across the congregation and into the distant skies beyond. In a moment the whites pulled Nat up with a jerk, but his body already seemed uninhabited —"Not a limb nor a muscle was observed to move," reported an eyewitness, as the Prophet hung there as still as stone. Afterward the authorities gave his body to surgeons for dissection. "They skinned it," according to William Sidney Drewry, "and made grease of the flesh."[41]

Nat was not the last Negro tried for the Southampton insurrection. On November 21, the court convicted Benjamin Blunt for complicity and he too was hanged. In 1832, the Southampton Superior Court witnessed the prosecution of four free Negroes charged with conspiracy and insurrection, found Barry Newsom guilty, and sentenced him to the gallows. In all, some fifty blacks stood trial in Southampton's courts, and twenty-one—including Nat Turner— were hanged. At the recommendation of the court, Governor Floyd apparently commuted the death sentences of ten other convicted slaves and ordered them transported—presumably out of the United States. At the same time, there were additional slave trials in several other counties in Virginia and North Carolina, resulting in twenty or thirty more executions. All told, Nat Turner's rebellion cost the lives of approximately sixty whites and more than two hundred Negroes.

As it turned out, several insurgents managed to avoid arrest and never came to trial. Whites suspected a few other blacks of collaboration and sold them off to Georgia. Also sold to slave traders were Nat's wife and daughter—though what happened to them after they left Southampton is not known. According to black tradition, one of Nat's sons remained in the county. And another, it was said, eventually found his way to the free state of Ohio.[42]

Part Four

LEGACY

The consequences of Nat Turner's insurrection did not end with public hangings in Virginia and North Carolina. For Southern whites the uprising seemed a monstrous climax to a whole decade of ominous events, a decade of abominable tariffs and economic panics, of obstreperous antislavery activities, and of growing slave unrest and insurrection plots, beginning with the Denmark Vesey conspiracy in 1822 and culminating now in the most lethal slave rebellion Southerners had ever known. Desperately needing to blame somebody for Nat Turner besides themselves, Southern whites inevitably linked the revolt to a sinister Northern abolitionist plot to destroy their cherished way of life. Southern zealots declared that the antislavery movement, gathering momentum throughout the 1820s, had now burst into a full-blown crusade against the South. In January, 1831, William Lloyd Garrison and Isaac Knapp had started publishing the *Liberator* in Boston, demanding in bold, strident editorials that the slaves be immediately and unconditionally emancipated. In a stunning display of moral indignation, Garrison said things most Southerners could not bear to hear. He upbraided slaveowners as unregenerate sinners of the most despicable sort. He insisted that Negroes deserved "life, liberty, and the pursuit of happiness" just like white people. He asserted that slavery violated the sacred ideals of the Declaration of Independence, made a mockery of Christianity, and exposed this hypocritical Republic to the severest judgments of Heaven. And while he pronounced his a pacifist crusade, Garrison warned that if Southerners did not eradicate slavery at once, then the blacks would fight for their freedom. "Woe," he had written in the very first issue of the *Liberator,* "if it comes with storm, and blood, and fire."

And now storm, blood, and fire had broken out in Virginia, and Southerners seized on the *Liberator* and held Garrison and his abolitionist cohorts responsible. Never mind that no evidence existed that Nat Turner had ever heard of Garrison. Never mind that no copies of his paper had been found anywhere in Southampton County. Southerners pointed out that about eight months after the appearance of the *Liberator* Nat Turner had embarked on his bloody venture—something Southern politicians, editors, and postmasters refused to accept as mere coincidence. They charged that Garrison and Knapp were behind the rebellion, that their "licentious," "traitorous," and "incendiary" rhetoric had incited Nat to violence. "These manifestoes of *Insurrection!*" howled one Virginia postmaster, who forwarded several confiscated issues of the *Liberator* to Floyd in Richmond. "These men do not conceal their intentions," the governor roared in reply, "but urge our negroes and mulattoes, slaves and free to the indiscriminate massacre of all white people."[1]

Shocked at such treachery, Floyd filed the issues of the *Liberator* in his "conspiracy" folder, along with a number of other antislavery documents allegedly found circulating in Virginia and sent to his office. There were copies of Walker's *Appeal* and Shadrack Bassett's "African Hymn." There were issues of *The Genius of Universal Emancipation,* published by the Quaker Benjamin Lundy. There was a copy of the *African Sentinel and Journal of Liberty,* put out by free Negroes in Albany, New York, with a quotation from Jefferson on its masthead: "I tremble for my country when I think that God is just, and that his justice cannot sleep forever!" And there were anonymous letters from the North which claimed that paramilitary operations were under way there, that bands of blacks and whites were "planning the massacre of the white people of the Southern states by the blacks." One letter, signed "Nero" of Boston and addressed to the Jerusalem postmaster, contended that Southampton whites got what they deserved and announced that not even "Your Nats and Harks" knew how widespread resistance to slavery really was.

For Floyd, these documents were both incriminating and profoundly revealing. Equally illuminating were all the letters falling on his desk about the activities of Northern vendors, free Negroes, and black preachers here in Virginia. And the more Floyd studied these communiqués, the more he compared the *Liberator* with Walker's *Appeal* and Bassett's hymn and the anonymous letters, the more convinced he became that a heinous Yankee conspiracy, with Garrison and Knapp as its "high priests" and Negro preachers as its Virginia agents, lay behind the Southampton uprising and all other slave troubles as well. And in November, in a sizzling letter to Governor Hamilton of South Carolina, Floyd sketched in the lurid details of the plot. "I am fully persuaded" that "the spirit of insubordination which has, and still manifests itself in Virginia, had its origin among, and eminated from, the Yankee population, upon their *first* arrival amongst us, but most especially the Yankee pedlars and traders." In covert, indirect fashion, these agents of revolution had enlisted the help of white evangelists and then embarked on the first step of their sordid plan: they made the blacks religious. They said to slaves that God was no respecter of persons, that the black man was as good as the white man. They said that all men were born free and equal. They said that men cannot serve two masters. They said that white people had rebelled against England to gain their freedom and "so had the blacks a right to do so." Thus, Floyd contended, the preachers—mostly Yankees—worked on our population "day and night" until religion became "the fashion of the times." Even white females from respectable Virginia families were persuaded that "it was piety to teach negroes to read and write, to the end that they might read the Scriptures." Many of these ladies became tutors in Negro schools and "pious distributors of tracts" from the New York Tract Society.

"At this point," Floyd went on, "more active operations commenced." As Virginia's magistrates and laws "became more inactive," the slaves held illegal religious meetings and permissive whites made little attempt to stop them. Then began the efforts of the black preachers, who circulated antislavery pamphlets and papers, read from their pulpits "the incendiary publications of Walker, Garrison and Knapp of Boston," and led their congregations in singing inflammatory hymns—"we resting in apathetic security until the Southampton affair."

From all the governor had learned about that affair, he was convinced that every Negro preacher east of the Blue Ridge Mountains was involved "in the secret" and acted on "the plans as published by those Northern presses." However, the congregations of these preachers "knew nothing of this intended rebellion, except a few leading and intelligent men, who may have been head men in the Church—*the mass* were prepared by making them aspire to an equal station by such conversations as I have related as the first step."

Once the rebellion succeeded, Floyd had been informed, the insurgents planned to adopt a form of government like that of the white people, "whom they intended to cut off to a man." The only difference was that "the preachers were to be their Governors, Generals and judges." Floyd was certain that "Northern incendiaries, tracts, Sunday Schools, religion and reading and writing has accomplished this end."

In Floyd's opinion, the situation had become intolerable. And the more he brooded about it, the more he fumed about that Boston "club of villains" and their wicked designs against his state, the more the governor focused his rage and resentment on one man— William Lloyd Garrison. Yes, Garrison was the chief scoundrel in this abysmal scenario of Yankee intrigue and infiltration—Garrison more than anybody else was to blame for the malicious slaughter of Virginia's men, women, and children. In righteous indignation, the governor demanded that Garrison be "silenced." He consulted with a Virginia judge about how "that fiend" might be crushed and punished, and the judge advised that Garrison might be prosecuted under common law. Floyd debated whether to "require" the governor of Massachusetts to have Garrison arrested. By now Floyd was in a tirade. Here Garrison was, a criminal, an agitator. Yet "we are told," Floyd gesticulated, that there are no laws to punish "Garrison's offense." No laws to punish his offense! A man in one state may "plot treason" against another state without fear of prosecution, yet the stricken state may not resist because the United States

Constitution does not provide for such resistance. *Damn* these constitutions (the governor was no strict constructionist when it came to suppressing abolitionists). There was a higher law which protected Virginia, Floyd announced, and that was "the law of nature," which "will not permit men to have their families butchered before their eyes by their slaves and not seek by force to punish those who plan and encourage them to perpetuate these deeds." He would bring this up in his message to the legislature, for "something must be done and with decision." He added: "If this is not checked it must lead to a separation of these States."[2]

Floyd's fulminations reveal more about his own anxieties—and those of Southern whites in general—than about the actual nature and influence of the Northern abolitionist movement. For one thing, Garrison and his followers were emphatically opposed to violence and said so repeatedly in the press and on the stump. They intended to overthrow slavery, not by insurrection, Northern interference, or coercive federal laws, but by converting public opinion and pricking the slaveholder's own conscience—whereupon, in a mighty burst of repentance, Southern whites were supposed to emancipate the slaves themselves.

Furthermore, the abolitionist movement was hardly so strong or well organized as Floyd and many other Southerners believed. As it happened, few Northerners—few Bostonians, for that matter—had ever heard of Garrison and his *Liberator* until Southerners raised such a fuss about them. Ironically enough, this dedicated pacifist rocketed to national attention because Southern whites accused him of inciting slave insurrections. Southerners, in short, made his reputation. But even so the circulation of the *Liberator* was never more than a few thousand, if that many; and most Northerners spurned the abolitionist movement itself as sinister and potentially destructive. Since the North was also a white supremacist society, the vast majority of whites there not only discriminated against free Negroes, but were perfectly content to leave slavery alone where it already existed. Many Northerners may have opposed slavery in the abstract, but most rejected actual emancipation—unless accompanied by wholesale colonization—lest abolition result in thousands of Southern blacks stampeding into the free states. In truth, racist feelings were so combustible in the North that ugly anti-abolitionist riots were to explode in various cities there.

Moreover, Northern public opinion was anything but sympathetic to slave resistance and rebellion. Though the Northern press was more concerned with national politics than with the Turner insurrection, many papers did report the news either in brief editorials or in excerpts from Southern journals. Apart from the small abolitionist press, few Northern papers blamed the Turner revolt on the South's own slave system—and those that did were mild in their criticism and generally advocated colonization. Other Northern papers not only castigated the Southampton insurgents, but promised Northern military assistance if Virginia needed it to suppress rebellions.[3]

Some Southern editors applauded the Northern reaction, contending that it demonstrated how impotent abolitionism was in the North and how powerful the ties of Union really were. But many other Southerners—perhaps most of them—agreed with Floyd's conspiracy thesis, and out of Dixie came a ground swell of outrage and protest against "the fanatical Garrison" and his abolitionist agents and allies. A Vigilance Association in Columbia, South Carolina, offered a $1,500 reward for any agitator convicted of distributing the *Liberator* or Walker's *Appeal*. In Raleigh and New Bern, North Carolina, grand juries indicted Garrison for violating a state law against circulating "incendiary" papers like his. The *Free Press* of Tarboro, North Carolina, had no doubt that the *Liberator* could be found among the slaves in every Virginia county and warned its readers: "Keep a sharp look out for the villains" who peddle that paper "and if you catch them, by all that is sacred, you ought to barbecue them." Another paper asserted that it was Garrison who ought to be barbecued. The Washington *National Intelligencer,* Richmond *Enquirer,* and many other Southern sheets demanded that the Boston authorities eliminate the "diabolical" *Liberator* and lock up its bloodthirsty editor. North Carolina even put a price of $5,000 on Garrison's head. And Georgia subsequently offered the same amount for anybody who would kidnap Garrison and drag him to Georgia for trial. Never mind legal rights and freedom of speech—in Southern eyes Yankee abolitionists didn't deserve any rights. Never mind the warnings of Baltimore's *Niles Register* that Southern whites, in their grasping for scapegoats, were attributing much too much influence to abolitionist literature. Never mind that Garrison, in the pages of the *Liberator,* declared himself "horror-struck" at the Southampton insurrection and hotly denied that he fomented slave rebellions ("Ye patriotic hypocrites! ye fustian declaimers for liberty! ye valiant sticklers for equal rights among yourselves! Ye accuse the pacific friends of emancipation of instigating the slaves to revolt. . . . The slaves need no incentive at our hands"). No matter what anyone said, anxious Southerners believed what they wanted to believe. From 1831 on, Northern abolitionism and slave rebellion were inextricably associated in the Southern mind.[4]

But if Virginians blamed the Turner revolt on Northern abolitionism, many of them—including Governor Floyd—defended emancipation itself as the only way to prevent further violence. In fact, for several months in late 1831 and early 1832 Virginians engaged in a momentous public debate over the feasibility of manumission. Out in the western part of the state, where antislavery and anti-Negro sentiment had long been smoldering, whites held public rallies in which they openly endorsed emancipation—yes, the liberation of all of Virginia's 470,000 slaves—as the only safeguard in these dangerous times. Whites in the extreme western counties had relatively few slaves anyway. Why should they support a dangerous slave regime that spawned violent "nigger" devils like Nat Turner? They sent a procession of memorials and petitions down to Richmond, demanding that Virginia extirpate the "accursed," "evil" slave system and colonize all blacks at state expense. Only by removing the entire Negro population, the petitions argued, could future rebellions be avoided.

At the same time, whites in the central piedmont and eastern tidewater also held meetings and drafted petitions. A majority of these blamed slave discontent on free Negroes and urged their removal. But opinion varied widely on the emancipation issue. Since the eastern tidewater had the heaviest slave concentrations, whites there generally defended the system, adopting proslavery positions that ranged from moderate to extreme. The tidewater planters, who possessed most of Virginia's wealth, power, and prestige and who dominated state politics, opposed abolition emphatically—and what they feared would amount to a radical reconstruction of Virginia's economy and social order. Other whites in central and eastern Virginia took a middle position: their petitions conceded that slavery might be an evil, but counseled against precipitous action in dealing with it. Nevertheless they insisted that the state government do something to ensure public safety.

Newspapers also joined in the debate, prompting the Richmond *Whig* to announce that "Nat Turner and the blood of his innocent victims have conquered the silence of fifty years." While many editors raged against manumission, young Pleasants of the *Whig* endorsed gradual emancipation at the very least. He editorialized that Virginia's large planters must understand—as the small slaveowner and the mechanic understood—that slavery was a curse on the state and that it must be expunged. Of course abolition could not be effected overnight; it would take time—a lot of time—before white prejudices could be overcome. Nevertheless, the big planters must eschew self-interest and help rid Virginia of slavery's "crushing and annihilating weight." For the institution emasculated the Old Dominion and the other Southern states as well, leaving them "an easy conquest at the feet of the North." Pleasants contended that the Northern states were gradually succumbing to abolitionism and predicted that one day they would strike against Southern slavery. So to avoid a sectional collision, Virginia must lead the way and remove the peculiar institution, thus freeing herself from conflicts that otherwise would inevitably come. If Virginia failed to do this, law and constitution would one day be forgotten and antagonisms over slavery would force "the strong hand to govern all," reducing Virginia to "the hewer of wood and the drawer of water" for the stronger Yankee states. In sum, only the blind and tempestuous could fail to foresee the calamities awaiting Virginia should slavery continue.[5]

While the Virginia press haggled over emancipation, Governor Floyd was plotting an executive move against the peculiar institution when the legislature convened in December. For some time he had desired emancipation and colonization, and now Nat Turner had given him a golden opportunity to strike against slavery, to vanquish what he regarded as a wasteful labor system that impeded Virginia's commercial development. Besides, Floyd wrote in his diary, removing slavery would thwart the abolitionists in the North, would "check the evil" there and disrupt all the intrigues of that dastard Garrison. On November 19 Floyd wrote Governor Hamilton of South Carolina that he favored gradual emancipation and colonization, but admitted that his plan "will of course be tenderly and cautiously managed, and will be urged or delayed as your state and Georgia may be disposed to cooperate." On November 21 Floyd announced to his diary: "Before I leave this Government, I will have contrived to have a law passed gradually abolishing slavery in this state, or at all events to begin the work by prohibiting slavery west of the Blue Ridge Mountains." He would propose some sort of abolition bill in his forthcoming message to the legislature.

But for some reason Floyd changed his mind and offered no emancipation scheme, none at all. For one thing, neither South Carolina nor Georgia—with their large percentage of blacks—would accept manumission on any terms. Also, Floyd was swept up in the national tempest over the tariff and South Carolina's drumbeat threats to nullify, over Jackson's "weak and wicked" administration and belligerent Unionist posturings, and over the upcoming Presidential election. These national issues may have convinced Floyd that the winter of 1831–1832 was not the proper time to push for gradual emancipation. In truth, John C. Calhoun himself may have talked the governor out of any abolition moves. On December 3, just before the legislature was to open, the Vice-President stopped over in Richmond on his way back to the national capital, dined and chatted with Floyd, and told him that South Carolina would nullify the tariff "unless it is greatly modified." Floyd recorded nothing else about their conversations, but Calhoun undoubtedly explained that South Carolinians too were upset about Nat Turner and blamed abolitionists like Garrison for inciting slave revolts. But Calhoun would never have approved of Floyd's emancipation ideas (and he was Floyd's hero), nor could the Vice-President have been happy about the public debates going on in Virginia. Surely Calhoun argued that the South could best protect its slave system from abolitionist coercion, not through emancipation, but behind a bulwark of state rights and nullification.[6]

Calhoun left for Washington on December 5, and the next day Floyd submitted his message to the legislature. In it, the governor said nothing about emancipation and colonization. He devoted most of the address to the Turner revolt, rehearsing the unsubstantiated charges that it sprang from a conspiracy of Northern "fanatics" and Negro preachers. To prevent any future uprisings, Floyd enjoined the legislature to outlaw these preachers, enact severe punishments against outside agitators, remove the state's free black population, rearm and strengthen the militia no matter what the cost, and create a new and special public guard, to consist of Virginia's best militiamen, which would drill once a month and be prepared to crush slave outbreaks at once. Military supremacy was imperative, Floyd declared, for "all communities are liable to suffer from the dagger of the murderer and midnight assassin," and it behooved all Virginia to guard against them.

Floyd devoted several paragraphs to his economic program, which called for state-subsidized internal improvements designed to make Virginia a magnificent commercial empire. Then he turned to "our FEDERAL RELATIONS" and unleashed a diatribe against federal despotism and the "unconstitutional measures" of the Jackson Administration. In language barbed with Calhounisms, the governor denounced the protective tariff as well as Jackson's proposal to distribute surplus national funds to the states, a proposal Floyd thought would favor states that exported nothing and discriminate against those like Virginia which exported a great deal. "The Constitution seems about to be merged in the will of an unrestrained majority," Floyd warned. "If the will of that majority is unrestrained, freedom is gone forever." He stoutly defended Calhoun's doctrines. "It is even now strongly insinuated, that the States cannot interpose to arrest an unconstitutional measure: if so, there is already no limit to Federal power, and our short experience has shewn us the utter insufficiency of all restraints upon parchment." If the Virginia legislature, however, took steps to guard against "unjust, oppressive and ruinous" federal measures, Floyd asserted, then "the strong arm of power will never be able to crush the spirit of freedmen, or deter them from exercising their rights and interposing barriers to the progress of usurpation."[7]

And that was that. In January, with Floyd looking on, the legislature plunged into a stormy debate over abolition and colonization, to last for several weeks, as proslavery and antislavery orators openly harangued one another. It was unprecedented in the South, this legislative struggle over manumission, and everybody involved realized what an exceptional event it was. "And what is *more remarkable* in the History of Legislation," observed Thomas Richie of the *Enquirer,* who boldly published the entire debates, is that "we now see the whole subject ripped up and discussed with open doors, and in the presence of a crowded gallery and lobby—Even the press itself hesitates to publish the Debates of the body. All these indeed [are] new in our history. And nothing else could have prompted them, but the bloody massacre in the month of August."

Outside Virginia, though, many Southern whites were appalled at Virginia's experiment in open discussion of abolition. Would this not arouse the slaves and terrify the white community even more? And was Richie not compounding the danger by printing the debates in his paper? In South Carolina, even the Unionists—those opposed to nullification—refused "to comment on a policy so unwise and blended with such madness and fatality." And the nullifiers, of course, were irate. They demanded that patrols go on the alert and castigated Richie as "the apostate traitor, the recreant and faithless sentinel, the cringing parasite, the hollow-hearted, hypocritical advocate of Southern interests" who "has scattered the firebrands of destruction everywhere in the South." Another Carolinian warned that publication of the debates was "calculated to unsettle everything—the minds of masters and slaves." And the Charleston *Mercury* concluded that "public discussion of such a topic . . . is fraught with evils of the most disastrous kind."

Meanwhile, up in Boston, William Lloyd Garrison followed the Virginia debates with sardonic glee. On January 14, 1832, he published in the *Liberator* a lively and sarcastic parody under the headline, "INCENDIARY SLAVEHOLDERS." "It seems that some of the slaveholders are imitating the example of the 'Incendiary' *Liberator* and actually discoursing about the gradual emancipation of their slaves. Strange that they wish to disturb so *embarrassing* a question! Strange that they pursue a course of conduct so well calculated to make their slaves *uneasy!* Certainly they ought to be indicted forthwith, and a reward of five thousand dollars offered for each of their heads." But "irony aside," Garrison was glad to see Virginians "in some measure brought to a sane state of mind" about slavery, although he considered gradual abolition "a delusion which first blinds and then destroys."

Blind or not, Virginia's legislators debated on through January and February, 1832, with antislavery spokesmen belaboring the Turner rebellion and the rampant hysteria that followed and stressing the destructive effects of slave labor. Proslavery orators, on the other hand, dismissed the Turner outbreak as "a petty affair," denied that slavery had caused Virginia's economic troubles, and insisted that property rights be thoroughly safeguarded. In the end, most delegates accepted the proslavery argument that colonization was too costly and too complicated to implement. And since they were not about to manumit the blacks and leave them as free people in a white man's country, they rejected emancipation. Indeed they went on to revise and implement the slave codes in order to restrict blacks so stringently that they could never again mount a revolt. The revised laws not only strengthened the militia and patrol systems, but virtually stripped free Negroes of human rights (a subsequent enactment prohibited any more from entering Virginia) and all but eliminated slave schools, slave religious meetings, and slave preachers. For Nat Turner had taught white Virginians a hard lesson about what might happen if they gave slaves enough education and religion to think for themselves.[8]

By now Governor Floyd had also capitulated, giving up any plans he might still have entertained about removing slavery from the Old Dominion. In April, 1832, he invited Professor Thomas R. Dew of William and Mary College, "an expert in whom all Virginia reposed the greatest confidence," to analyze the recent debates and publish his conclusions and recommendations. A leading spokesman for the tidewater proslavery forces, Dew happily accepted the job and went on to produce his *Review of the Debate of the Virginia Legislature of 1831 and 1832* (Richmond, 1832), which contained the most comprehensive vindication of slavery to emerge from the South thus far. In the *Review,* Dew mounted an all-out assault on western Virginia's gradual emancipationists, contending that colonization was impossible and that abolition without it was heresy. Negroes, Dew argued, copulated and reproduced so prodigiously that no colonization scheme could ever get rid of them all: as soon as one batch was transported, two other batches would be born. Then Dew got down to vindications. Slavery was *not* an evil as Jefferson's generation had tended to believe, but was a necessary stage of human progress. Moreover, from sheer practical considerations, the institution was an indispensable means of regulating Negroes, who were "not ready" for freedom. Indeed, Negroes were "vastly inferior" to whites and should not be liberated. The professor hinted that Negroes were innately indolent and that no free black would work unless you made him. But racial arguments aside, Negroes were accustomed to being slaves—had acquired all the habits and outlooks of bondsmen —and whites were used to being masters. Dew insisted that these prejudices had solidified in Virginia and that the state could not legislate such prejudices away.

When Dew's essay came out, Governor Floyd and most other Virginia whites embraced the professor's arguments "as final." If Nat Turner had forced Virginians, however fleetingly, to consider black liberation as a solution to their slave woes, Dew gave them a fund of excuses and rationalizations for their rejection of that possibility. Given their racial fears and attitudes, their investments and status symbols, their whole way of life really, Virginia whites were incapable of ever uprooting slavery by themselves. Small wonder, then, that they closed ranks behind Dew and dug in, inflexibly determined that slavery would remain. Thanks to white intransigence and to those oppressive new codes, Virginia's blacks were more shackled to the rack of slavery than they had ever been.[9]

The years that followed were fateful ones for the South. In 1832 South Carolina fire-eaters triumphed in crucial state elections and went on to nullify the tariff as they had threatened to do. That year Congress had enacted another tariff which removed some of the abominations of 1828, but not enough to mollify the nullification party. In November, 1832, with John Floyd cheering them on in Richmond, South Carolina nullifiers held a convention in Charleston and declared both the tariffs of 1828 and 1832 null and void. Invoking the theory of state sovereignty contained in Calhoun's

Exposition and Protest and in Jefferson's *Kentucky Resolutions* of 1798, the nullifiers moved to erect a state-rights barricade behind which to protect South Carolina's slave regime from all forms of federal "despotism." But Andrew Jackson would have none of it; in a ringing manifesto to the people of South Carolina, the President denounced nullification as incompatible with the very concept of Union. But South Carolina flung defiance at Old Hickory, mobilized a volunteer force "to defend the rights and liberties of the State," and raced pell-mell down the road to secession. The President, encouraged by support from all sections of the country (including the South), threatened to hang Calhoun and vowed to hurl an army into South Carolina to enforce the tariff. For a time it looked as though civil war would break out between the federal government and South Carolina. Should that happen, Governor Floyd warned the Virginia House of Delegates, then "the days of this Republic are numbered." Anxious to avoid a bloody showdown, Jackson favored a compromise and so did Congress, which produced a bill calling for the gradual reduction of tariff duties. Congress also enacted a force bill empowering Jackson to use federal troops in the crisis. As it happened, the South Carolina convention accepted the lower tariff and rescinded its nullification ordinance, only to turn around and nullify the Force Act in a show of bluster and pugnacity. South Carolinians thus reasserted the *right* of nullification because they were still obsessed with Northern abolitionism. As Jackson himself predicted, "The next pretext will be the Negro, or slavery question."

In the wake of Nat Turner and the rise of the abolitionists, the other Southern states also expanded their patrol and militia systems and increased the severity of their slave codes to maintain internal security. For the South seemed increasingly beset with provocation and danger. In 1833 Northern abolitionists formed the American Antislavery Society, whose task was to coordinate the activities of all abolitionist groups and organizations and to disseminate books, sermons, and pamphlets in an effort to convert all America to emancipation. At the same time, the British government enacted a gradual abolition law and obstreperous English emancipators came to crusade in the United States as well. What followed was the Great Southern Reaction of the 1830s and 1840s, a time when the Old South, menaced it seemed by internal slave disaffection and outside abolitionist agitation, became a closed, martial society determined to preserve and perpetuate its slave-based civilization come what may. To prevent any national emancipation law (and to rally proslavery support at home), Southern leaders in Washington sought to squelch antislavery protest and to control and manipulate the federal government itself. In the Southern states postmasters began confiscating abolitionist literature, lest these tracts invite more slaves to violence. And Southern zealots set about suppressing internal dissent as well. Across Dixie vigilance committees seized "abolitionist," "anti-Southern" books and burned them. They expelled from classrooms any teacher suspected of abolitionist tendencies, and ostracized or banished anybody who questioned the peculiar institution. Some states actually passed sedition laws and other restrictive measures which prohibited whites and blacks alike from criticizing slavery. In sum, the Old South became a suspicious and repressive community which made defense of slavery "the *sine qua non* of Southern patriotism."

Because the South seemed more and more a lonely slave outpost surrounded by antislavery enemies, Southern spokesmen in the period of the Great Reaction produced a strident vindication of slavery that went beyond Thomas Dew's celebrated defense. To counter the abolitionist cry that slavery was sinful, Southerners increasingly proclaimed that institution a positive and unequivocal good, condoned by the Bible and ordained by God from the beginning of time. "Negro slavery," asserted James H. Hammond of South Carolina, "is the greatest of all the great blessings which a kind providence has bestowed." John C. Calhoun, having resigned as Vice-President and returned to Washington as a United States Senator, trumpeted the glories of slavery on the floor of the Senate itself. Pronouncing slavery "a good—a positive good," he flayed away at Northern abolitionists, warning that the peculiar institution was absolutely essential for race control and that it could not be subverted "without drenching the country in blood, and extirpating one or the other of the races." He went on to justify slavery on broad historical grounds, insisting that "there never has yet existed a wealthy and civilized society in which one portion of the community did not, in point of fact, live on the labor of the other." Other Southerners, citing contemporary science and anthropology, argued that Negroes were an inferior race and therefore belonged in chains as naturally as cattle in pens. Slavery, Southern whites contended, "civilized" the barbaric African because it taught him a trade and made him productive and obedient. As it turned out, Southerners were doing Negroes a huge Christian favor by enslaving them.

Out of mixed feelings of fear and racial superiority, Southern whites created their own image of the Negro as a submissive, feeble-minded Sambo, that "banjo-twanging, hi-yi-ing happy jack" who abounded in antebellum Southern literature. Yet as Southerners told themselves and the rest of the world that their darkies were too docile and too content ever to turn against their chivalrous masters, they still took every necessary precaution to prevent another insurrection, whether incited by mutinous slaves or infiltrating Yankees. By the 1840s, with its repressive slave controls, police measures, and toughened military forces, the Old South had devised a slave system oppressive enough to make organized rebellion all but impossible.[10]

Even so, Southern whites in the antebellum period never forgot Nat Turner and the violence he unleashed in southeastern Virginia. For some whites, such as Nathaniel and Lavinia Francis, the revolt was a cataclysmic occurrence by which to measure time itself. When their baby was born, they recorded in the family Bible that the child arrived "one month and six days after the insurrection."[11] The revolt marked Governor Floyd, too, for it turned out to be the most significant event of his administration. Having failed to remove slavery from Virginia or to guide the Old Dominion into a golden new era of economic enterprise (though the state's economic condition did improve some in the 1830s), Floyd left office in 1834 and retired to Montgomery County, where he suffered a paralytic stroke and died in 1837.

Meanwhile pamphlets about the insurrection had begun to appear, reminding white readers all over again about the grisly details of Nat's work. The first pamphlet, compiled by one Samuel Walker and published in New York in October, 1831, was a long-winded tract culled largely from newspapers.[12] That November a Baltimore printer brought out Gray's *Confessions of Nat Turner,* which sold well enough to merit a second printing in 1832. All told, the *Confessions* sold about forty thousand copies, although some Southern communities appear to have suppressed it, presumably because of its "incendiary" character. (Indeed, Garrison himself remarked that a bounty should be placed on Gray's head, because the *Confessions* might "hasten other insurrections.") The Richmond *Enquirer* praised Gray for producing a graphic and revealing document, but chastised him for its style. "The language is far superior to what Nat Turner could have employed—Portions of it are even eloquently and classically expressed." This attributed to "the Bandit a character for intelligence which he does not deserve, and ought not to have received." But in most other respects the *Enquirer* found the *Confessions* "faithful and true" and thought "it ought to warn Garrison and the other fanatics of the North how they meddle with these wretches."[13]

In truth, fear of such "wretches" haunted Southern whites throughout the rest of the antebellum period. In spite of all their precautions and all their resounding propaganda, they could never escape the possibility that somewhere, maybe even in their own slave quarters, another Nat Turner was plotting to rise up and slit their throats. His name became for them a symbol of black terror and violent retribution.[14]

But for antebellum blacks—and for their descendants—the name of Nat Turner took on a profoundly different connotation. He became a legendary black hero—especially in southeastern Virginia, where blacks enshrined his name in an oral tradition that still flourishes today. They regard Nat's rebellion as the "First War" against slavery and the Civil War as the second. So in death Nat achieved a kind of victory denied him in life—he became a martyred soldier of slave liberation who broke his chains and murdered whites because slavery had murdered Negroes. Nat Turner, said an elderly black man in Southampton County only a few years ago, was "God's man. He was a man for war, and for legal rights, and for freedom."[15]

EPILOGUE:
SOUTHAMPTON COUNTY, 1973

During the summer of 1973, after I had completed the archival and library research on Nat Turner, I went to Southampton County in order to visit the landmarks of Nat's life, to walk in his footsteps and sense his world. It was an unforgettable experience for me and indispensable for the preparation of this book. Indeed, being on the ground gave me a feel for Nat Turner country—a sense of the land, forests, smells, and the people both black and white—that I could not otherwise have acquired. Several Turner-era houses still stood in 1973, serving as rustic shrines to Southampton's single most important historical event. And local blacks, of course, have commemorated the rebellion in other ways, from oral reminiscences to lore and legend. Old Percy Claud of Boykins can tell folk stories that will keep you on the edge of your chair. And Herbert Turner claims to be a descendant of Nat, though his father—dead five years now—knew more about the family connection and about Nat himself than Herbert remembers. An articulate man in his fifties, Herbert Turner operates a country store and is co-owner of the land where Phipps captured Nat that October Sunday of 1831.

Accompanied by my wife, Ruth, I arrived in Southampton on Sunday, July 15, and spent a couple of days poking around Jerusalem—it's called Courtland now—and gathering impressions of the county. We quickly learned that whites and blacks were still separated by a strict racial caste system at the same time that they were bound inextricably together. We discovered, too, what little white officialdom had done to preserve the memory of Nat Turner. Near an intersection just west of Courtland, in some weeds off the side of U.S. Highway 58, stood this terse marker.

SOUTHAMPTON INSURRECTION
Seven miles southwest Nat Turner, a
Negro, inaugurated, August 21, 1831, a
slave insurrection that lasted two
days and cost the lives of about sixty
whites. The slaves began the massacre
near Cross Keys and moved eastward
towards Courtland (Jerusalem). On
meeting resistance, the insurrection
speedily collapsed.

We stared at that marker—especially the last sentence—for a long time. Then Ruth said, "Not quite like the statues in Richmond, is it."

When our preliminary scoutings were done, we called on an attorney in Boykins, a member of the Southampton County Historical Society who might help us locate Turner materials. It was a sweltering July afternoon when we drove into Boykins, a sleepy whistlestop down near the North Carolina line, close to where Cross Keys once was located. Dogs were languishing in the gutters and whites and blacks were going their separate ways on the sidewalks of Main Street, which is that segment of Highway 35 which passes through town. Still, the seventies have not entirely overlooked Boykins: a bearded young black, wearing sunglasses, rumbled around us in a red Mustang. As we parked our car and waited to cross the street, an old International pickup stopped to let us pass; the driver —a white man—stuck his head out of the cab and said with a huge grin, "We got manners—even in Boykins!"

We found the lawyer's office on Main Street, a comfortable office in modern decor with a reception room and a book-lined chamber in back where he worked at his desk. Suntanned and in his forties, the attorney is courteous, fashionably dressed, and well educated, with a law degree from the University of Virginia. He will tell you

148

straight off that he is a liberal—an Adlai Stevenson liberal—and that he subscribes to the *Center Magazine,* published by the Center for the Study of Democratic Institutions in California. He has a thriving practice, representing as many blacks as whites, and in fact relates to Negroes with genuine concern (we had barely arrived when a Negro man came to see him about a legal matter, and I watched as they talked). Moreover, he serves as a sort of liaison between whites and blacks in the county. Being a liberal in the rural South is not an easy life, and he is careful to conform to certain accepted ways (he attends the Baptist church, belongs to the historical society) and to work within the strictures and established institutions of the white community. He was born in Boykins and has lived here all his life. As we chatted over coffee, his son came in—he is a tall youngster with hair long like a rock singer's. After he had gone, we got down to business: before the attorney would cooperate in my work on Turner, he subjected me to a lawyer's cross-examination about my own politics, previous books, and approach to history and writing. More or less satisfied with my views, he then opened his family papers and agreed to get me into the documents room in the county courthouse (I knew I would need help before coming to Southampton). But he announced in no uncertain terms that Southampton's white establishment—especially the all-white historical society—would not be interested in my book on Nat Turner, in what I thought about the man, or the rebellion, or Southampton County, because I was an outsider from Massachusetts. Worse still, I was born and raised in the Texas Panhandle—the frontier—and therefore had no "religion," "traditions," or "family roots."

I found out what he meant when we met later at the courthouse in Courtland. A clerk in the courthouse—a woman—bristled when we were introduced: she clearly did not want outsiders messing around in her documents and stirring up the ghost of Nat Turner. Even the lawyer conceded that she was "sensitive" on this score. He spoke with her, though, and then ushered me quietly into the documents room. But all the while I was there the woman kept an eye on me from the front office.

After I had finished at the courthouse, Ruth and I planned to retrace the entire course of the insurrection, from the beginning at Cabin Pond to the end at Nat's forlorn cave. I was particularly eager to visit the old houses—those of Giles Reese, Caty Whitehead, Richard Porter, Peter Edwards, William Williams, Rebecca Vaughan, and Simon Blunt—in hopes that they would transport me back into Nat's world, back into the rebellion he led. We set out around two o'clock on a hot still cloudy afternoon, equipped with beer, sandwiches, writing pads, and maps and photographs. We drove south on Highway 35, heading back to Boykins, Ruth jotting down my impressions as I muttered them, my eye a camera that zoomed and focused on the landscape around me. Southampton is as forested and rolling now as it was in Nat's time, with oceanic cornfields flooding the meadows and clearings. The farms seem endless repetitions of white frame houses and rough-hewn barns and sheds. With all the windows rolled down, we slow the Dodge to a wagon's pace, entranced with half-forgotten smells wafting in from the farms and fields—smells of hay and wild grasses and vegetable patches. The air is humid and profoundly still, so that we can hear the cry of a bird—the bellow of a cow—from deep in the forests. I imagine us in an open wagon, on a slow, jingling ride from Jerusalem's fly-infested market back to Joseph Travis's farm northwest of Cross Keys. . . . But a gasoline truck roars around us, disturbing the image. Presently we reach Boykins, plot our course on a county map, and head northwest into the backwoods, climbing up a forested incline toward the clouds.

For a half-hour we are lost in a maze of county roads, scouting north on some graveled trace, doubling back on a road that is more weed than pavement. But at last we find it—the remote neighborhood where Joseph and Sally Travis, Benjamin and Samuel Turner, Giles Reese, Caty Whitehead, Nathaniel and Lavinia Francis all lived. As in Nat's time, it is an area of dense thickets and swamps, of meadows that meander through communities of trees and then sweep away into the forests beyond. Suddenly the woods are so thick that trees crowd against the road, their limbs reaching over and obscuring the sky. Emerging from the forests into a grassy meadow, we come upon a Negro shack, hooked to the road by a path, and the blacks on the porch look no different and no better off than slaves. An old black man is sitting in a rocking chair on the porch, but he does not rock. It is too hot to rock. Children stand like stair steps to his right, as still as cranes in danger. Beyond the shack thunderheads are moving in, threatening a storm. In a moment we pass another antebellum dwelling, where silhouettes of Negroes are visible at the edges of doors and windows, watching as we drive by.

In time we come to a sandy intersection, park the car in some weeds, and make our way through a cornfield to Giles Reese's tumbledown cabin. A small place, only a couple of rooms, with the windows all boarded up now. Nearby is an even more decrepit shanty—maybe the slave quarters where Cherry and the children slept. Standing inside, swatting away the gnats and flies, one is stricken with the realization that 1831 was really only yesterday.

Back on the road, we descend on the site of the Travis farm, where the rebellion began in earnest. Alas, the house is gone now, in its place another rural Southern home with a car and a pickup parked in front. On again, past sandy fields that have spilled onto the road, we locate a graveled trace called County Road 667, scanning a wooded knoll that conceals Caty Whitehead's place. Much as the insurgents might have done, we approach it by a path winding up from the road below. A scraggly tree guards the house like a sentry. It is beginning to drizzle, I standing in the garden near the front of the abandoned building, with its yawning porch, twin chimneys, and skull-eye windows. Once the "big house" on the Whitehead plantation, it is similar to the plain two-story farmhouses out on the prairies of Texas and Kansas. The space between the chimneys where Margaret hid herself is camouflaged by a tree in summer blossom. Here Nat found her as he ran by. Here she cried out and fled for her life, Nat in close pursuit, both pounding down the slope in back of the house, to act out a tragic tableau in one of the fields there.

In motion again, racing inexorably along the back roads, the momentum of the insurrection carrying us faster now, we pass through a narrow opening in the woods and by some miracle of time the Richard Porter house comes hurtling out of 1831 . . . or we go hurtling back . . . and there is bedlam in the lane ahead of us—insurgents on skittish horses, the slave Venus rattling on about how her white folks is gone, Nat riding off to retrieve the infantry. . . . But the image passes. The Porter house is a skeleton, a haunted gray relic of time. Bales of hay are stacked in the kitchen and living room; crows flutter and caw upstairs. The chimneys move precariously against the clouds.

As we followed behind Will and the insurgent cavalry, moving along a sandy road from Porter's to Nathaniel Francis's place, a thunderstorm broke over the area, and the clouds crashed and rolled overhead, and lightning splintered the sky like glass, and the wind pummeled the fields and forests in angry gusts, I watching all the while for signs of tornadoes (I lived through one as a boy)—for tails hanging along the cloud line against the sky. In a moment rain came raking across the land, driven on by wind and murderous thunder. The storm moved away as rapidly as it struck, leaving the area to boil in the sun. We traveled north at the speed of galloping horses, following a road that rose and dipped, rose and dipped, through redundant forest groves. At last we came to a vast cornfield which, according to my maps and photographs, contained the old Francis house. I parked the car and got out. "Don't you want to go?" I asked Ruth. She said no, she would wait in the car. All our talk about the rebellion and the remoteness here in the backwoods had left her unsettled. "Sure you won't go?" I asked. She was sure— but she locked both doors when I left.

When I came to Nathaniel's house on the edge of the corn, I stood rooted to the spot as the wind moaned through the deserted rooms, as though it were looking for something lost. It was a mysterious shell of a house, with its knocked-out windows and interior wreckage, spangled now with spiderwebs. Yet as I stood there in the weeds, scanning the broken steps and the ruptured hallway and the unhinged doors and the sagging stairs inside, the place seemed *inhabited* . . . every room a museum of memories. And for a moment I could have sworn I smelled the aroma of freshly baked bread . . . yes, and the stench of manure from Nathaniel's stock pens. And then I could hear Nathaniel talking to pregnant young Lavinia in the kitchen there, could hear his nephews playing in the forest sanctuary in back of the house, could smell the acrid scent of cedar logs and see the slaves out in the fields beyond, singing those powerful spirituals that had moved me to tears to write about. And then—was that the sound of plunging hooves after all?—there was a frightful clamor in front of the house. And Will and Sam and the other horseback insurgents swept into the yard, leaped from their mounts, and broke into the house with axes; and I could hear the gunshots and the decapitated cries of dying people; I became one of Francis's slaves who stood in inert terror in the shade of the barn, all the while Frederick Douglass's words echoed like thunder in my head (all are brutalized, all) . . . and then I ran, I ran all the way back up the path to where my car was parked, and my wife, seeing me running up, had a look of fear on her face as real as what I felt inside.

We followed the insurgents to Peter Edwards's house, a stark ruins off in the distance from the road. We rode with them along the entire stretch of the Barrow Road, witnessed the killings at William Williams's and Rebecca Vaughan's, engaged the whites in Parker's cornfield south of Jerusalem, got ambushed at Simon Blunt's plantation, and fell back into hiding in the gloomy woods around Cabin Pond. Afterward, driving back along the Barrow Road (now County Road 658), we stopped one last time at Rebecca Vaughan's house, situated back in the trees behind a field. A John Deere tractor and a couple of plows stood incongruously in the yard, the very yard where the rebels had formed a circle and shouted at Rebecca as she pleaded with them from behind the windowpanes. One last time I stood on the porch, listening to the echoes of August, 1831.

As we drove back along the sandy trail, a dark-blue sedan bore down on us from the direction of the Barrow Road, and the dread rose in us again. It turned out to be two blacks—a man and a woman—who forced us to pull over. The woman was big and menacing. "You lookin' for somebody?" She had her door open. "I said you *look*in' for somebody?" In her fright, Ruth turned to me and asked if we were looking for somebody. Though I did not want to, I got out of the car and went over to talk. The man wore a short-brimmed white straw hat, was thin and maybe in his late twenties, and had an inscrutable expression on his face. The woman, though, was glowering; and I began to understand why. This was black property. Evidently her family had lived in the area a long time and that was their tractor and plows up at the Vaughan house; and I guess they thought that I, a white boy, had come here to syphon gas or steal something else. I explained that I was a writer down here doing a book on Nat Turner . . . from Massachusetts . . . and had simply wanted to have a look at the old Vaughan place. "You doin' a book on Nat Turner?" the woman asked. And her hostility subsided into ordinary suspicion. She checked out my car plates—asked me a few questions about Massachusetts—and then relaxed a little. She said her mother owned one of the farms further down the road, but she didn't live with her mother no more—lived up in New York now. Visited here in the summers was all. She knew about Nat Turner, a lot about him. Her mother had a magazine down at the house with an article—pictures—on the rebellion. You know about his wife? I said I did, yes. Herbert Turner—owns Turner's store?—you know he's a relative of Nat's. Yes, I replied, I knew. She said I could come to the house and see the magazine if I wanted. But I was too shaken to go, made some wretched excuse, said good-bye, asked her name, said good-bye (she answered cordially enough, the man stared at the corn), got in the car and drove away. "Jesus," Ruth sighed. "Let's go back to the motel." In the rear-view mirror I saw the blue sedan parked at the Vaughan house, the two blacks looking around.

Later, in another part of the county, we stopped at a bank to cash a check. A bank official—a small, nervous fellow in loafers, a pink shirt, and matching burgundy suit and tie—came out to approve my credentials. When he found out we were from New England and were doing research on Nat Turner, he flew into an impromptu monologue about Southampton's "colored problem," gesturing emphatically with a cigarette. "Why I know a lot of boys, do business with them, talk with them on the street. But you can't go socializin' with boys less you want to get ostracized. Sure we got problems here—not denyin' it. But you got to understand, people won't change what they believe overnight. We got boys and girls here bright enough—not sayin' we don't. Had a girl while back even went off to college. Won a prize in a Shakespeare play. Talked like Pres'dent Kennedy used to talk, but come back and fell back to talkin' like they all do." He paused to scrawl his initials on my check. "No sir, can't change things overnight." He gave my check to the teller and smiled as we parted. "Come back and see us, hear now?"

REFERENCE NOTES

Along with Nat's own *Confessions* to Thomas R. Gray, discussed in the text, Southampton County's slave trial records constitute one of the major sources for Nat's rebellion and are indispensable for an understanding of it. The original trial records are located in the Minute Book of the Southampton County Court (1830–1835), pp. 72–146, which is preserved in the Southampton County Courthouse in Courtland (formerly Jerusalem). The trial records are printed verbatim in Henry Tragle's compilation of documents, described below. For the convenience of readers, all of my citations are to the slave trial transcripts as reproduced in Tragle's volume. In addition, contemporary accounts written by Jerusalem residents and published in several Virginia and North Carolina newspapers are invaluable historical documents. I am thinking in particular about the long communiqué of September 17, 1831, which appeared in the Richmond *Whig* of September 26, 1831, and which I analyzed in the text. As I said there, internal evidence strongly suggests that Attorney William C. Parker of Jerusalem was the author. Other illuminating on-the-spot reports appeared in the *Whig*, the Richmond *Enquirer*, the Richmond *Compiler*, and the Raleigh *Register*, all of which I cite in the notes.

The Archives of the Virginia State Library in Richmond house a number of vital materials that bear on the insurrection. These include John Floyd's Diary, Governor's Papers, Executive Letterbook, and Free Negro and Slave Letterbook of 1831; Virginia State Executive Communications (December 5, 1831, to March 9, 1833), the Journal of the Governor's Council (1828–1831), the Journal of the House of Delegates (1831), Southampton County's Personal Property Tax Lists (which I consulted from 1797 to 1832), and the Papers of the Virginia State Auditor's Office, Item #153, Box #14, which, among other things, contains a wealth of data on the Virginia militia units used to suppress the insurrection. The Virginia State Library also has microfilm copies of pertinent county court records, such as Southampton's Deed Books, Will Books, and the Minute Book of the Southampton Court itself. The original county documents, of course, are kept in the courthouse in Courtland, as are Southampton County's Superior Court Orders (1832), Guardian Accounts, and Marriage Register (Old Series), 4 volumes, 1750–1853. Official transcripts of slave trials conducted beyond Southampton are located in the Isle of Wight Court Order Book (1830–1834), Isle of Wight, Virginia; in the Sussex County Court Orders (1827–1835), Sussex, Virginia; and in the Surry County Court Orders (1829–1833), Surry, Virginia.

For North Carolina and the rebellion, the Department of Archives in Raleigh has several essential collections. Among these are the Papers of Pattie Mordecai and Benajah Nicholls, which contain letters that are germane to the insurrection, and the Governors' Papers and Letterbooks of John Owen and Montford Stokes. In addition to some miscellaneous manuscripts cited in the notes, I have used the John Floyd Papers in the Archives of the Library of Congress and the U.S. Census Returns for Virginia and Southampton County, 1810, 1820, and 1830, in the National Archives, Washington, D.C.

Of the published sources and books about the rebellion, by far the most valuable is Henry Irving Tragle (ed.), *The Southampton Slave Revolt of 1831* (Amherst, Mass., 1971), a collection of documents about virtually all aspects of the Turner story. Not only are the Southampton slave trial records gathered here, but so are numerous contemporary newspaper reports, selections from Governor Floyd's Diary and correspondence, and most of the previously published accounts, including Nat's original *Confessions* to Gray, printed in Baltimore in 1831. Again, for the convenience of researchers, all of my references are to the *Confessions* as published in Tragle's work. I am also indebted to Eric Foner, whose *Nat Turner* (Englewood Cliffs, N.J., 1971), another compilation of source materials, caused me to dig deeper into the role of the slave church in the genesis of the Turner revolt. On the significance of slave religion and the slave underground in the Turner story, I have benefited considerably from the essays by Vincent Harding and Mike Thelwell in John Henrik Clarke (ed.), *William Styron's Nat Turner: Ten Black Writers Respond* (Boston;

1968), 23–33, 79–91. I have also drawn from the previous book-length treatments of the rebellion: William Sidney Drewry, *The Southampton Insurrection* (reprint of the 1900 ed., Murfreesboro, N.C., 1968); Herbert Aptheker, *Nat Turner's Slave Rebellion* (paperback ed., New York, 1968); and F. Roy Johnson, *The Nat Turner Slave Insurrection* (Murfreesboro, N.C., 1966), and *The Nat Turner Story* (Murfreesboro, N.C., 1970). My debts to other historians and editors are indicated in the specific references that follow.

PROLOGUE: SOUTHAMPTON COUNTY, 1831

1. To compare Southampton's slaveholding statistics with those for the South at large, see Kenneth M. Stampp, *The Peculiar Institution: Slavery in the Ante-Bellum South* (New York, 1956), 27–33. My sketch of Southampton's class structure and economic and social conditions derives from the U.S. Census Returns for 1830, Southampton County, Virginia; *Documents Containing Statistics of Virginia* (Richmond, 1851), Table IV; Southampton County's Personal Property Tax Lists, 1825–1831, for such individuals as Thomas Ridley, James Parker, Giles Reese, John Kelly, Richard Porter, Peter Edwards, Levi Waller, Jn. Urquhart, Sr., and many others; and Arthur G. Peterson, *Historic Study of Prices Received by Producers of Farm Products in Virginia, 1801–1927* (Bulletin #37, Virginia Polytechnic Institute, March, 1929), 20ff. See also Aptheker, *Nat Turner's Slave Rebellion,* 14–15; Tragle, *Southampton Slave Revolt,* 14–15; and Drewry, *Southampton Insurrection,* 20–22, 103–108.

2. Unsigned letter from Jerusalem, September 17, 1831, in Richmond *Whig,* September 26, 1831; John Floyd to Governor James Hamilton of South Carolina, November 19, 1831, Floyd Papers, Library of Congress; Floyd's Message to the Virginia Legislature, December 6, 1831, Journal of the House of Delegates (Richmond, 1831), Archives of the Virginia State Library (and printed in Tragle, *Southampton Slave Revolt,* 430–444); N. Sutton to Floyd, September 21, 1831, Virginia Governors' Papers, Archives of the Virginia State Library; unsigned letter to Floyd [November, 1831], *ibid.*; Foner, *Nat Turner,* 3; Works Progress Administration, *Negro in Virginia* (Hampton, Va., 1940), 109.

PART ONE: THIS INFERNAL SPIRIT OF SLAVERY

1. Benjamin Turner, Personal Property Tax Lists for 1800–1810, Archives of the Virginia State Library; Benjamin Turner's Will and the inventory and appraisal of his property, Southampton County Will

Books, VII, 107–109, 167–169; Nat Turner's *Confessions* in Tragle, *Southampton Slave Revolt,* 306; Drewry, *Southampton Insurrection,* 27; Johnson, *Nat Turner Insurrection,* 18, and *Nat Turner Story,* 38. See also Tragle, *Southampton Slave Revolt,* 411, and Mary Booth Healey, The Family of Nathaniel Francis of Southampton County, Virginia, typescript in possession of Gilbert Francis of Boykins, Virginia.

2. My profile of Benjamin Turner's family was put together from Turner's Personal Property Tax Lists for 1797–1810; the Wills of Simon Turner, William Turner, and Benjamin Turner (father of the Benjamin Turner who owned Nat), Southampton County Will Books, I, 410–413, II, 152, and III, 333; Benjamin Turner's own Will and the inventory and appraisal of his property, *ibid.,* VII, 109–110, 167–169, 189 (Turner's Will was made out on December 28, 1805, and was recorded on October 16, 1810); Southampton County Deed Books, XII, 189, 244–246; and Johnson, *Nat Turner Insurrection,* 11–17, and *Nat Turner Story,* 17–21, 28.

3. The sketch of the early Methodists and slavery draws from Francis Asbury, *The Heart of Asbury's Journal* (ed. by Ezra Squier Tipple, New York and Cincinnati, 1904), 172; Donald G. Mathews, *Slavery and Methodism: A Chapter in American Morality, 1780–1845* (Princeton, N.J., 1965), 3–29; Emory Stevens Bucke and others, *History of American Methodism* (3 vols., New York and Nashville, 1964), I, 252–256; Luther P. Jackson, "Religious Instruction of Negroes," *Journal of Negro History,* XV (January, 1930), 72–114; and Herbert Aptheker, *American Negro Slave Revolts* (new edition, New York, 1969), 103.

4. Black tradition about Nat's mother, Nancy, is related in Johnson, *Nat Turner Story,* 29; Drewry, *Southampton Insurrection,* 27; and Lucy Mae Turner, "The Family of Nat Turner, 1831 to 1954," *Negro History Bulletin,* XVIII (March, 1955), 128. Lucy Mae Turner, who says she is Nat's granddaughter, writes that Nat's mother was reported to have been of royal African blood. John W. Cromwell, "The Aftermath of Nat Turner's Insurrection," *Journal of Negro History,* V (April, 1920), 208–209, and William Wells Brown, "The Nat Turner Insurrection," in *The Negro in the American Rebellion* (Boston, 1867), 19, both contend that Nat's father was also a full-blooded African, so that Nat was "of unmixed African descent." That Nat's mother may have become a house servant is suggested by the fact that she passed into the hands of Samuel Turner, who willed her and two other domestic slaves to his wife, Elizabeth. See Southampton County Will Books, IX, 134.

5. Quotations and information about Nat's boyhood from Nat Turner's *Confessions* in Tragle, *Southampton Slave Revolt,* 306–307, 316; unsigned letter from Jerusalem, August 24, 1831, in Richmond *Enquirer,* August 30, 1831; and Drewry, *Southampton Insurrection,* 27, 115. Though Thomas R. Gray, in an epilogue to Turner's *Confessions,* states that Nat's parents taught him to read, Nat himself made no such claims, remarking that somehow he just learned ("I have no recollection whatever of learning the alphabet"). Anyway it seems unlikely that Nat's African-born mother ever became literate. On this score, see Johnson, *Nat Turner Insurrection,* 189–190, and Seymour L. Gross and Eileen Bender, "History, Politics and Literature: The Myth of Nat Turner," *American Quarterly,* XXIII (October, 1971), 508–509.

6. Nat Turner's *Confessions* in Tragle, *Southampton Slave Revolt,* 308. John Cromwell said that Nat's father eventually went to Liberia, but Tragle, *ibid.,* 388, could find no evidence that this is so.

7. My profile of Samuel Turner is based on Southampton County Deed Books, XI, 346, and XIV, 81–83; Southampton County Guardian Accounts, 82, 83; Southampton County Will Books, VII, 109, 167–169, and IX, 134, 190, 254; U.S. Census Returns for 1810, Southampton County, Virginia; and Samuel Turner, Personal Property Tax Lists for 1809 and 1810. On religious instruction as a means of slave discipline, see W.P.A., *Negro in Virginia,* 108–109; Jackson, "Religious Instruction of Negroes," *Journal of Negro History,* XV, 72–114; Aptheker, *American Negro Slave Revolts,* 56–58; John Blassingame, *The Slave Community: Plantation Life in the Ante-Bellum South* (New York, 1972), 61–63; and George P. Rawick, *From Sundown to Sunup: the Making of the Black Community* (Westport, Conn., 1972), 36.

8. My description of white fears of slave unrest and rebellion before 1800 draws from Gerald W. Mullin, *Flight and Rebellion: Slave Resistance in Eighteenth-Century Virginia* (New York, 1972), 54–78, 124–135; Thomas Wentworth Higginson, "Gabriel's Defeat," in *Black Rebellion* (new edition, New York, 1969), 83; Blassingame, *Slave Community,* 117–118; Drewry, *Southampton Insurrection,* 118–125; and Aptheker, *American Negro Slave Revolts,* 41–45, 162–219, 238. Because Aptheker's volume is based largely on the records and newspapers of white people, it may or may not be an accurate record of legitimate slave resistance and rebellion. I regard the book, though, as a valuable guide to white rumors and anxieties about their slaves. For an assessment of Aptheker, see Kenneth M. Stampp, "Rebels and Sambos: the Search for the Negro's Personality in Slavery," *Journal of Southern*

History, XXXVII (August, 1971), 369–370. On the slave grapevine, see, for example, Rawick, *Sundown to Sunup,* 107–108. John Quincy Adams, *Works,* II, 428, remarked that "The Negroes have a wonderful art of communicating intelligence among themselves; it will run several hundreds of miles in a week or a fortnight."

9. William P. Palmer and others (eds.), *Calendar of Virginia State Papers* (11 vols., Richmond, 1875–1893), IX, 51–52; Drewry, *Southampton Insurrection,* 111–112; and Aptheker, *American Negro Slave Revolts,* 211–219.

10. Mullin, *Flight and Rebellion,* 140–169; Aptheker, *American Negro Slave Revolts,* 219–228; Monroe to Jefferson, September 5, 1800, in the *Writings of James Monroe* (ed. by S. M. Hamilton, 7 vols., New York and London, 1898–1903), III, 201; Robert Reid Howison, *A History of Virginia* (2 vols., Philadelphia, 1846–1848), II, 393–394; and Winthrop D. Jordan, *White Over Black: American Attitudes Toward the Negro, 1550–1812* (paperback ed., Baltimore, 1969), 542–569.

11. See Aptheker, *American Negro Slave Revolts,* 234–257.

12. My paraphrase of the apologetic "necessary evil," but "keep-it-quiet" defense of slavery derives from William S. Jenkins, *Pro-Slavery Thought in the Old South* (Chapel Hill, N.C., 1935), 3–48; Robert McColley, *Slavery and Jeffersonian Virginia* (Urbana, Ill., 1964), 114–132; Jordan, *White Over Black,* 542–582; Staughton Lynd, "The Abolitionist Critique of the U.S. Constitution," in Martin Duberman (ed.), *The Antislavery Vanguard* (Princeton, N.J., 1968), 218–239; Charles G. Sellers, Jr., "The Travail of Slavery," in Sellers (ed.), *The Southerner as American* (Chapel Hill, N.C., 1960), 40–71; Howison, *History of Virginia,* II, 389–390; and Stampp, *Peculiar Institution,* 3–27. See also William W. Freehling, "The Founding Fathers and Slavery," *American Historical Review,* LXXVII (February, 1972), 81–93. Basil Hall, who toured the South in 1827 and 1828, thought slaveholders regarded slavery as an evil, but considered abolition "so completely beyond the reach of any human exertions" that emancipation was the "most profitless of all possible subjects of discussion."

13. Samuel Turner, Personal Property Tax Lists for 1809–1813; Southampton County Marriage Register (Old Series), II, entry of May 27, 1818; Johnson, *Nat Turner Story,* 49.

14. Appraisal of Samuel Turner's property in Southampton County Will Books, IX, 254. A native of Virginia described a slave boy's coming of age as "the dawn of the first bitter consciousness of being a slave," and Lunsford Lane agreed. M. D. Conway's statement in Aptheker,

American Negro Slave Revolts, 54, and Lane, *Narrative* (Boston, 1848), 7–8. Those who describe Nat as a skilled slave are wrong. In 1822, Nat was valued at $400—the price of a good field hand. During his trial for insurrection, he was valued at only $375. By contrast, a slave blacksmith also tried for the rebellion was valued at $675. Moreover, Nat mentions nothing in the *Confessions* about ever being a skilled slave; rather, he refers to himself as a field hand at work behind his plow.

15. My sketch of slave life is based on Blassingame, *Slave Community,* 41–103; Rawick, *Sundown to Sunup,* 3–13, 53–119; Frederick Douglass, *My Bondage and My Freedom* (paperback ed., New York, 1969), 104–105, *Narrative* (paperback ed., New York, 1968), 31–36, 84, and *Life and Times* (new paperback ed., London, 1962), 165–167; W.P.A., *Negro in Virginia,* 67–70; Drewry, *Southampton Insurrection,* 24–25, 105–108; Sterling Stuckey, "Through the Prism of Folklore: the Black Ethos in Slavery," *Massachusetts Review,* IX (Summer, 1968), 417–437; Lawrence W. Levine, "Slave Songs and Slave Consciousness: An Exploration in Neglected Sources," reprinted in Allen Weinstein and Frank Otto Gatell (eds.), *American Negro Slavery* (2d ed., New York, 1973), 153–182. I have also consulted Robert William Fogel's and Stanley L. Engerman's *Time on the Cross: The Economics of American Negro Slavery* (Boston, 1974), especially 106–157, which deal with slave families and slave life and labor. While many of the authors' points are valuable indeed, their generalization that slave courtships and marriages were largely paragons of Victorian virtue seems highly questionable and unsupported by quantifiable evidence, the kind the authors purport to use throughout their volume. Blassingame, who in *The Slave Community* already offered several of the arguments and correctives contained in *Time on the Cross,* asserts that slaves had only an imperfect understanding of the Victorian moral code and escaped much of the sexual inhibition that marred a good many white people of that time. Unfortunately for me, Eugene D. Genovese's *Roll, Jordan, Roll: The World the Slaves Made* (New York, 1974) appeared after my volume had gone to press. But I have consulted his other writings, particularly "American Slaves and Their History," *New York Review of Books* (December 3, 1970), 34–43.

16. Nat Turner's *Confessions* in Tragle, *Southampton Slave Revolt,* 307; Southampton County Guardian Accounts, 82, 83; unsigned letter from Jerusalem, September 17, 1831, in Richmond *Whig,* September 26, 1831.

17. Quotation about Nat's observant mind and material about his religious concerns from Nat Turner's *Confessions* in Tragle, *Southampton Slave*

Revolt, 307. Drewry, *Southampton Insurrection,* 115, also found that Negro preachers enhanced Nat's sense of self-importance. My description of the slave church and slave religion draws from James L. Smith (a skilled slave shoemaker in Virginia in 1831), *Recollections* (Norwich, Conn., 1881), 26–30; Foner, *Nat Turner,* 2, 176–177; Aptheker, *American Negro Slave Revolts,* 55–59; Blassingame, *Slave Community,* 64-76; Rawick, *Sundown to Sunup,* 30–52; and the essays by Harding and Thelwell in Clarke (ed.), *William Styron's Nat Turner,* 25–26, 27–29, 80–81, as well as Harding's "Religion and Resistance Among Ante-Bellum Negroes, 1800–1860," in August Meier and Elliott Rudwick (eds.), *The Making of Black America* (New York, 1969), I, 179–197.

18. Nat Turner's *Confessions* in Tragle, *Southampton Slave Revolt,* 307–308. See also unsigned letter from Jerusalem, September 17, 1831, in Richmond *Whig,* September 26, 1831; unsigned letter from Jerusalem, August 24, 1831, in Richmond *Enquirer,* August 30, 1831; and unsigned letter from Southampton, October 31, 1831, in Richmond *Whig,* November 7, 1831.

19. Nat Turner's *Confessions* in Tragle, *Southampton Slave Revolt,* 308. On Samuel Turner, see Southampton County Deed Books, XVI, 171, 197; U.S. Census Returns for 1820, Southampton County, Virginia; and Samuel Turner's Personal Property Tax Lists for 1819–1821. Physical description of Nat is from William C. Parker to Governor John Floyd, September 14, 1831, Virginia State Executive Communications, Archives of the Virginia State Library; Gray's epilogue to the *Confessions* in Tragle, *Southampton Slave Revolt,* 317; unsigned letter from Jerusalem, September 17, 1831, in Richmond *Whig,* September 26, 1831; and unsigned letter from Southampton, November 1, 1831, in Richmond *Enquirer,* November 8, 1831.

20. Nat Turner's *Confessions* in Tragle, *Southampton Slave Revolt,* 308; Tragle's chronology, *ibid.,* xv; and Douglass, *Narrative,* 76. Thelwell, in Clarke (ed.), *William Styron's Nat Turner,* 86, conjectures that Nat may have run away and then returned "simply to establish his trustworthiness" among his slave followers, "thereby getting the mobility necessary to organize."

21. On Nat's wife see the unsigned letter from Jerusalem, September 17, 1831, in Richmond *Whig,* September 26, 1831; Raleigh *Register,* September 3, 1831 (containing a letter from a Jerusalem lawyer who reported that, "from accounts of his wife," Nat had plotted insurrection since 1828); Thomas Wentworth Higginson, "Nat Turner's Insurrection," *Black Rebellion,* 168, drawing from contemporary newspapers; Samuel Warner's 1831 pamphlet about the rebellion, also

based on contemporary newspapers, in Tragle, *Southampton Slave Revolt,* 296; and Tragle, *ibid.,* 13, 160, 327; Johnson, *Nat Turner Story,* 55, and *Nat Turner Insurrection,* 179. Contemporary accounts do not mention the name of Nat's wife, but evidently it was Cherry Turner. According to Southampton County Court records, Cherry resided on Samuel Turner's place in 1822 and became the property of Giles Reese at the time that Nat was sold to Thomas Moore. Samuel Warner, culling information from newspapers, reported that Nat's wife still lived with Reese in 1831. Which makes perfect sense, because Nat bypassed the Reese place when the rebellion began. Since Cabin Pond (where the insurgents planned the massacres) was located on Reese's land and since the Reese cabin was an easy target, Nat undoubtedly spared the man because his wife and children resided with him.

22. Southampton County Will Books, IX, 134, 254; Southampton County Deeds, XXII, 161; Douglass, *Narrative,* 59–60; Blassingame, *Slave Community,* 70–73. For Nat's family, see sources cited in the previous note, plus Drewry, *Southampton Insurrection,* 28, and Lucy Mae Turner, "Family of Nat Turner," *Negro History Bulletin,* XVIII, 127–132. According to Lucy, Nat had a daughter and a son named Gilbert (Lucy's father) who subsequently obtained his freedom and made his way to Ohio. Drewry contends that Nat had another son, named Redic, who remained in Southampton and that many of Nat's descendants were still there in the 1890s. Herbert Turner, of course, resides there today.

23. My profile of Thomas and Sally Moore is based on Southampton County Marriage Register (Old Series), II, 281; Southampton County Deeds, XXIX, 6, 29; Southampton County Will Books, IX, 194, 254; Thomas Moore's Personal Property Tax Lists for 1819–1822; U.S. Census Returns for 1820, Southampton County, Virginia; Healey, Family of Samuel and Sally (Powell) Francis, typescript in possession of Gilbert Francis, Boykins, Virginia.

24. Quotation (Nat was an "all-purpose chattel") from William Styron, *Confessions of Nat Turner* (paperback ed., New York, 1968), 262; quotation ("he had a mind capable of attaining anything") from Gray's epilogue to Nat Turner's *Confessions* in Tragle, *Southampton Slave Revolt,* 317; Nat's growing self-esteem and corresponding sense of resentment and alienation from his slave world in his own *Confessions, ibid.,* 307–309, in John Hampden Pleasants's account in Richmond *Whig,* September 3, 1831, and in the unsigned letter from Jerusalem, September 21, 1831, in Richmond *Enquirer,* September 27, 1831; and Lane, *Narrative,* 8.

PART TWO: GO SOUND THE JUBILEE

1. Nat Turner's *Confessions* in Tragle, *Southampton Slave Revolt*, 308–309; Southampton County slave trial records in *ibid.*, 222; unsigned letter from Southampton, November 1, 1831, in Richmond *Enquirer*, November 8, 1831; unsigned letter from Jerusalem, September 17, 1831, in Richmond *Whig*, September 26, 1831; unsigned letter from Southampton, October 31, 1831, in *ibid.*, November 7, 1831.

2. Nat Turner's *Confessions* in Tragle, *Southampton Slave Revolt*, 309; unsigned letter from Jerusalem, August 24, 1831, in Richmond *Enquirer*, August 30, 1831; unsigned letter from Southampton, September 4, 1831, in Richmond *Whig*, September 8, 1831; Pleasants's account in *ibid.*, September 3, 1831; unsigned letter from Jerusalem, September 17, 1831, in *ibid.*, September 26, 1831; unsigned letter from Jerusalem, August 31, 1831, in Richmond *Compiler*, September 3, 1831; and Drewry, *Southampton Insurrection*, 26, 30–32. The antebellum Baptist church had "colored members who were accounted as preachers," reported one church historian (Johnson, *Turner Insurrection*, 46), but who were not officially licensed. The Baptists likewise employed whites as lay or "farmer" preachers.

3. Drewry, *Southampton Insurrection*, 28, 32–33, 114; Nat Turner's *Confessions* in Tragle, *Southampton Slave Revolt*, 308; unsigned letter from Jerusalem, September 17, 1831, in Richmond *Whig*, September 26, 1831; unsigned letter from Jerusalem, September 21, in Richmond *Enquirer*, September 27, 1831.

4. Nat Turner's *Confessions* in Tragle, *Southampton Slave Revolt*, 309; Southampton County slave trial records in *ibid.*, 222; unsigned letter from Jerusalem, September 21, 1831, in Richmond *Enquirer*, September 27, 1831; unsigned letter from Southampton, November 1, 1831, in *ibid.*, November 8, 1831; unsigned letter from Jerusalem, September 17, 1831, in Richmond *Whig*, September 26, 1831; unsigned letter from Southampton, October 31, 1831, in *ibid.*, November 7, 1831; Drewry, *Southampton Insurrection*, 27–28; quotation ("commissioned by Jesus Christ") from unsigned letter from Jerusalem, August 24, 1831, in Richmond *Enquirer*, August 30, 1831. On the 1826 drought see the letters from Virginia in New York *Evening Post*, May 30 and July 19, 1826, and Aptheker, *American Negro Slave Revolts*, 120.

5. Nat Turner's *Confessions* in Tragle, *Southampton Slave Revolt*, 309–310; unsigned letter from Jerusalem, September 21, 1831, in Richmond *Enquirer*, September 27, 1831; and Drewry, *Southampton Insurrection*, 33n.

6. Nat Turner's *Confessions* in Tragle, *Southampton Slave Revolt*, 310;

Southampton County slave trial records in *ibid.*, 222; unsigned letter from Jerusalem, September 17, 1831, in Richmond *Whig*, September 26, 1831; unsigned letter from Southampton, November 1, 1831, in Richmond *Enquirer*, November 8, 1831, reporting Nat's court interrogation of October 31; letter from a Jerusalem lawyer in Raleigh *Register*, September 3, 1831.

7. My account of the Vesey conspiracy and subsequent insurrection scares in South Carolina draws heavily from William W. Freehling, *Prelude to Civil War: The Nullification Controversy in South Carolina, 1816–1836* (New York, 1966), 49–86; and John Oliver Killens (ed.), *Trial Record of Denmark Vesey* (Boston, 1970). See also Aptheker, *American Negro Slave Revolts*, 268–276, and John Lofton, *Insurrection in South Carolina* (Yellow Springs, Ohio, 1964).

8. Freehling, *Prelude to Civil War,* 89ff; McColley, *Slavery and Jeffersonian Virginia,* 114–125; Lynd, "Abolitionist Critique of U.S. Constitution," in Duberman, *Antislavery Vanguard,* 218–239; Charles S. Sydnor, *Development of Southern Sectionalism, 1819–1848* (Baton Rouge, La., 1948), 177–202.

9. Christian Tompkins to John Floyd, July 18, 1829, Governors' Papers, Archives of the Virginia State Library; Journal of the Virginia Governor's Council (1828–1829), 138–139, *ibid.;* T. M. Whitfield, *Slavery Agitation in Virginia, 1829–1832* (Baltimore, 1930), 54; Drewry, *Southampton Insurrection,* 116; and Aptheker, *American Negro Slave Revolts,* 82, 283–285.

10. Walker's *Appeal* (reprint of original 1829 ed., New York, 1969), 11–88.

11. Raleigh *Register,* November 18, 1830; James McRae to Governor John Owen, August 7, 1830, North Carolina Governors' Letterbooks, XXVIII, 218–219, North Carolina Department of Archives; Aptheker, *American Negro Slave Revolts,* 31–33, 81–83, 265, 281–292; Drewry, *Southampton Insurrection,* 123–124, 152; and Sydnor, *Development of Southern Sectionalism,* 222–224.

12. See Floyd to Hamilton, November 19, 1831, Floyd Papers, Library of Congress; unsigned letter from Jerusalem, September 17, 1831, in Richmond *Whig,* September 26, 1831; and numerous letters in late August, September, and October, 1831, in the Governor's Papers of John Floyd, Archives of the Virginia State Library, complaining about white permissiveness before Nat Turner.

13. Tragle, *Southampton Slave Revolt,* 17–20; Aptheker, *American Negro Slave Revolts,* 67–68, 291; John Hope Franklin, *Militant South* (paperback ed., Boston, 1964), 171–192; and William E. Dodd, *The Old South Struggles for Democracy* (New York, 1937), 105.

14. Most reports from Southampton described the shock and disbelief whites felt in the wake of Turner's rebellion: since they thought their slaves were well treated, they could not fathom why any would rebel. See the unsigned letter from Jerusalem, September 17, 1831, in Richmond *Whig,* September 26, 1831; Pleasants's account in *ibid.,* September 3, 1831; Gray's introduction to Nat Turner's *Confessions* in Tragle, *Southampton Slave Revolt,* 303–304; and Drewry, *Southampton Insurrection,* 20ff.

15. Unsigned letter from Jerusalem, September 17, 1831, in Richmond *Whig,* September 26, 1831. Drewry, *Southampton Insurrection,* 113, claimed that Nat read "the newspapers and every book within his reach," but there is no evidence that he read Walker.

16. My sketch of Joseph Travis and of Nat's relationship with him derives from Nat's *Confessions* in Tragle, *Southampton Slave Revolt,* 310; Travis's Personal Property Tax Lists for 1828–1831; Southampton County Will Books, XI, 353–354; Southampton County Marriage Register (Old Series), III, entry on October 5, 1829; U.S. Census Returns for 1830, Southampton County, Virginia; Healey, Family of Nathaniel Francis, typescript in possession of Gilbert Francis, Boykins, Virginia. Drewry, *Southampton Insurrection,* 28–31, erroneously asserts that at Travis's Nat became a Negro overseer and a skilled slave. See note #14 of Part One above.

17. Nat's *Confessions* in Tragle, *Southampton Slave Revolt,* 310; Nat's court interrogation of October 31, 1831, as reported in unsigned letter from Southampton, November 1, 1831, in Richmond *Enquirer,* November 8, 1831, and in unsigned letter from Jerusalem, October 31, 1831, in Richmond *Whig,* November 7, 1831.

18. During the Southampton slave trials, Nat and his lieutenants were valued at the price of prime field hands—Hark at $450, Nelson at $400, Sam at $400, and Nat at $375. We do not know Henry's value. My profiles of the four lieutenants and account of their plottings with Nat from February to August, 1831, are from Nat's *Confessions* in Tragle, *Southampton Slave Revolt,* 310; Southampton County slave trial records in *ibid.,* 191–198; Nat's court interrogation of October 31, 1831, as reported in unsigned letter from Jerusalem, October 31, 1831, in Richmond *Whig,* November 7, 1831 (Nat said he "dreaded" to commence), and in unsigned letter from Southampton, November 1, 1831, in Richmond *Enquirer,* November 8, 1831; unsigned letter from Jerusalem, September 17, 1831, in Richmond *Whig,* September 26, 1831; *ibid.,* September 1, 1831; Norfolk *American Beacon,* August 27, 1831; Raleigh *Star,* September 3, 1831; and Drewry, *Southampton Insurrection,* 34, 35n, 60, 99, 116–117. Whites contended that at least

six free blacks were in on Nat's plannings—among them Billy Artis and Barry Newsom. Both joined the revolt in progress.

19. Richmond *Enquirer,* September 2, 1831; Richmond *Whig,* August 22, 1831; Richmond *Compiler,* August 13, 1831; Raleigh *Star,* August 18 and 25, 1831; unsigned letter from Jerusalem, August 24, 1831, in Richmond *Enquirer,* August 30, 1831; Pleasants's account in Richmond *Whig,* September 3, 1831; unsigned letter from Jerusalem, September 17, 1831, in *ibid.,* September 26, 1831; Southampton County slave trial records in Tragle, *Southampton Slave Revolt,* 222; and Nat's *Confessions* in *ibid.,* 310.

20. Scene one: Pleasants's report from Jerusalem, August 25 and 27, 1831, Richmond *Whig,* August 29, 1831, and Drewry, *Southampton Insurrection,* 157. Scene two: Southampton County slave trial records in Tragle, *Southampton Slave Revolt,* 214–215; unsigned letter from Jerusalem, September 21, 1831, in Richmond *Enquirer,* September 27, 1831; Sussex County slave trial records, Sussex County Court Orders (1827–1835), 248–256; Johnson, *Nat Turner Insurrection,* 127–128. Scenes three and four: Southampton County slave trial records in Tragle, *Southampton Slave Revolt,* 193, 202–203.

21. See Foner, *Nat Turner,* 177.

22. Copy of "African Hymn" in Floyd's Free Negro and Slave Letterbook, Archives of the Virginia State Library; George Cooke to Floyd, September 13, 1831, Virginia Governors' Papers, *ibid.;* N. Sutton to Floyd, September 21, 1831, *ibid.;* "A Friend to the City" to Floyd [November, 1831], *ibid.;* and Richmond *Enquirer,* September 17, 1831.

PART THREE: JUDGMENT DAY

1. My profile of John Floyd is based on Floyd's Diary, entries of March 8, April 29, June 29, August 21 and 22, October 10, November 10 and 21, 1831, Archives of the Virginia State Library; Floyd's Message to the Legislature, December 6, 1831, in Journal of the House of Delegates (Richmond, 1831), *ibid.* (and printed in Tragle, *Southampton Slave Revolt,* 430–444); Floyd on education and U.S. Senators in Floyd to [?], May 5, 1832, Floyd Papers, Library of Congress; Floyd's defense of nullification in his communication to the Speaker of the Virginia House of Delegates, December 13, 1832, Virginia Executive Letterbooks, Archives of the Virginia State Library; Charles H. Ambler, *Life and Diary of John Floyd* (Richmond, 1918), 87ff; Tragle, *Southampton Slave Revolt,* 249–250; W. H. T. Squires, *Through Three Centuries, A Short History of the People of Virginia* (Portsmouth, Va., 1929), containing a portrait of Floyd, 414–419.

2. Quotation ("mean son-of-a-bitch") Styron, *Confessions,* 108, 113; my sketch of Nathaniel and Lavinia Francis is based on U.S. Census Returns for 1830, Southampton County, Virginia; Healey, Family of Samuel and Sally Francis and Family of Nathaniel Francis, typescripts in possession of Gilbert Francis, Boykins, Virginia; portrait of Nathaniel in possession of *ibid.;* Nathaniel Francis's Personal Property Tax Lists for 1828–1831; Southampton County Deed Books, XXI, 495; Tragle, *Southampton Slave Revolt,* 163 (containing a picture of Lavinia taken from Drewry), 410–411; Drewry, *Southampton Insurrection,* 43, 46–48; my interview with Gilbert Francis, Boykins, Virginia, July 16, 1973.

3. Drewry, *Southampton Insurrection,* 25–26; Johnson, *Nat Turner Insurrection,* 79.

4. William Wells Brown, *Negro in the American Rebellion,* 23, paints the fictional sketch of Will. Brown's account also includes invented speeches.

5. My description of the meeting at Cabin Pond draws from Nat's *Confessions* in Tragle, *Southampton Slave Revolt,* 310–311; Southampton County slave trial records in *ibid.,* 195–196, 197; Nat's court interrogation of October 31, 1831, as reported in his trial, *ibid.,* 222, and in unsigned letter from Jerusalem, October 31, 1831, in Richmond *Whig,* November 7, 1831, and unsigned letter from Southampton, November 1, 1831, in Richmond *Enquirer,* November 8, 1831; unsigned letter from Jerusalem, September 17, 1831, in Richmond *Whig,* September 26, 1831; Pleasants's account in *ibid.,* September 3, 1831; unsigned letter from Jerusalem, August 31, 1831, in Richmond *Compiler,* September 3, 1831; Norfolk *Herald,* November 4, 1831; and Drewry, *Southampton Insurrection,* 22–23, 25–26, 56, 113. Nat's ultimate objectives may never be known. Afterward, some Jerusalem residents speculated that the insurgents hoped to fight their way to Norfolk, seize a ship, and sail away to Africa (Pleasants's report from Jerusalem, August 25 and 27, 1831, in Richmond *Whig,* August 29, 1831). Higginson, "Nat Turner's Insurrection," *Black Rebellion,* 174, reports that Nat intended to "conquer Southampton County as the white men did in the Revolution, and then retreat, if necessary, to the Dismal Swamp." Drewry, *Southampton Insurrection,* 113, conjectures that Nat desired to capture Southampton County, storm into the Dismal Swamp, and eventually take over the whole state of Virginia, "as the Americans had the British in the Revolutionary War," all to "call the attention of the civilized world to the condition of his race." As I suggest in the text, Nat possibly thought that God would interfere and guide the course and destiny of the rebellion. Pleasants in the *Whig,*

September 3, 1831, observed that Nat may have expected divine assistance. Similarly, Henry Tragle, "The Southampton Slave Revolt," *American History Illustrated*, VI (November, 1971), 8, points out that the lack of preparations suggests that Nat saw himself as an instrument of vengeance in the hands of Jehovah. And that is certainly the spirit Nat conveys in the *Confessions* themselves. Still, his final objectives remain obscure. The author of the unsigned letter of September 17, 1831, correctly states that one of Nat's main goals was to conquer Jerusalem [with its Biblical symbolism?] and massacre the inhabitants, but beyond that "he gave no clue to his design."

6. Nat's *Confessions* in Tragle, *Southampton Slave Revolt*, 311; Southampton County slave trial records in *ibid.*, 196, 220; Nat's court interrogation of October 31, 1831, as reported in *ibid.*, 222, and in unsigned letter from Jerusalem, October 31, 1831, in Richmond *Whig*, November 7, 1831, and in unsigned letter from Southampton, November 1, 1831, in Richmond *Enquirer*, November 8, 1831; Pleasants's account in Richmond *Whig*, September 3, 1831; unsigned letter from Jerusalem, September 17, 1831, in *ibid.*, September 26, 1831; and unsigned letter from Jerusalem, August 31, in Richmond *Compiler*, September 3, 1831.

7. From the Travis place to Elizabeth Turner's: Nat's *Confessions* in Tragle, *Southampton Slave Revolt*, 311–312; Southampton County slave trial records in *ibid.*, 185, 186, 195; Drewry, *Southampton Insurrection*, 38–42, 91n.

8. Whitehead massacre: Southampton County slave trial records in Tragle, *Southampton Slave Revolt*, 179–182, 185–186, 207; Nat's *Confessions* in *ibid.*, 312, 318; unsigned letter from *Jerusalem*, September 17, 1831, in Richmond *Whig*, September 26, 1831; F. M. Capehart to Benajah Nicholls, August 23–26, 1831, Benajah Nicholls Papers, North Carolina Department of Archives; Drewry, *Southampton Insurrection*, 42–44. I assume that Hark, as second in command, led the group on foot that attacked the Bryant family. My chronology of the early hours of the revolt differs in some particulars from that in Tragle, *Southampton Slave Revolt*, xvi–xvii.

9. From the Whitehead place through the attack on Nathaniel Francis's: Nat's *Confessions* in Tragle, *Southampton Slave Revolt*, 312, 318; Southampton County slave trial records in *ibid.*, 180, 200–201; Norfolk *Herald*, September 3, 1831; Capehart to Nicholls, August 23–26, 1831, Nicholls Papers, North Carolina Department of Archives; Drewry, *Southampton Insurrection*, 45–48, 118; Johnson, *Nat Turner Story*, 38, 101.

10. From the Francis place through the rendezvous at the Harris planta-

tion on the Barrow Road: Southampton County slave trial records in Tragle, *Southampton Slave Revolt,* 196, 208, 217–218; Nat's *Confessions* in *ibid.,* 312–313, 318; unsigned letter from Jerusalem, August 24, 1831, in Richmond *Enquirer,* August 30, 1831; unsigned letter from Jerusalem, September 17, 1831, in Richmond *Whig,* September 26, 1831; Pleasants's account in *ibid.,* September 3, 1831; Drewry, *Southampton Insurrection,* 44–45, 50–55.

11. Southampton County slave trial records in Tragle, *Southampton Slave Revolt,* 189–190, 202, 203, 223; James Trezevant's report in Journal of the Virginia Governor's Council, August 23, 1831, Archives of the Virginia State Library, and described in Richmond *Compiler,* August 24, 1831, and Richmond *Whig,* August 25, 1831; Drewry, *Southampton Insurrection,* 66, 76, 89.

12. My profile of Levi Waller is based on U.S. Census Returns for 1830, Southampton County, Virginia; Waller's Personal Property Tax Lists for 1830–1831; and Drewry, *Southampton Insurrection,* 56. My account of the killings at Waller's was put together from the Southampton County slave trial records in Tragle, *Southampton Slave Revolt,* 178, 194, 198, 218, 221–222; Nat's *Confessions* in *ibid.,* 313, 317–318; unsigned letter from Jerusalem, August 24, 1831, in Richmond *Enquirer,* August 30, 1831; and Pleasants's report from Jerusalem, August 25 and 27, 1831, in Richmond *Whig,* August 29, 1831. My version of the massacre differs somewhat from those in Drewry, *Southampton Insurrection,* 56–59, and in Johnson, *Nat Turner Insurrection,* 93–95.

13. Unsigned letter from Jerusalem, September 17, 1831, in Richmond *Whig,* September 26, 1831; Drewry *Southampton Insurrection,* 87–88; Levi Waller's petition for compensation (certified by A. P. Peete, November 22, 1831, and eyewitnessed by Thos. Porter on the same day) in Papers of the Virginia State Auditor's Office (Item #153, Box #14), Archives of the Virginia State Library.

14. Attacks on Williams and Vaughan homesteads and Nat's behavior on the Barrow Road: Nat's *Confessions* in Tragle, *Southampton Slave Revolt,* 313; Southampton County slave trial records in *ibid.,* 193–194, 195; Pleasants's report from Jerusalem, August 25 and 27, 1831, in Richmond *Whig,* August 29, 1831; Pleasants's account in *ibid.,* September 3, 1831; and Drewry, *Southampton Insurrection,* 59–62.

15. From the rendezvous at the Barrow Road-Jerusalem highway intersection to the encampment at Ridley's plantation: Southampton County slave trial records in Tragle, *Southampton Slave Revolt,* 178, 183, 194–195, 203–204, 220–221; Nat's *Confessions* in *ibid.,* 313–315; Richmond *Compiler,* August 29, 1831; unsigned letter from Jerusalem, August 31, 1831, in *ibid.,* September 3, 1831; unsigned letter from

Jerusalem, September 17, 1831, in Richmond *Whig,* September 26, 1831; U.S. Census Returns for 1830, Southampton County, Virginia; Drewry, *Southampton Insurrection,* 62–70; and Johnson, *Nat Turner Story,* 82. Contrary to what several writers have said, I could find no evidence that Jerusalem had an arsenal.

16. Journal of the Virginia Governor's Council, August 23, 1831, Archives of the Virginia State Library; Floyd's Diary, August 23, 1831, and Floyd's Message to the Legislature, December 6, 1831, Journal of the House of Delegates, in *ibid.;* Floyd to Brigadier-General Richard Eppes, August 25 and 31, 1831, and Floyd to James H. Gholson, August 24, 1831, Virginia Executive Letterbooks, *ibid.;* Richmond *Compiler,* August 24, 1831; Richmond *Enquirer,* August 26, 1831; Richmond *Whig,* August 25 and 29, 1831; Petersburg *Intelligencer,* August 26, 1831; Norfolk *American Beacon,* August 26, 1831; Baltimore *Niles Register,* August 26, 1831; Richmond *Times,* January 25, 1891; Lester J. Cappon, *Virginia Newspapers, 1821–1935* (New York and London, 1936), 192–194; William "Box" Brown, *Narrative* (Boston, 1849), 37–40; *The Liberator* (Boston), October 1, 1831; Tragle, *Southampton Slave Revolt,* 16–17, 23; and Drewry, *Southampton Insurrection,* 75–77.

17. Capehart to Nicholls, August 23–26, 1831, Nicholls Papers, North Carolina Department of Archives; John D. Pipkin to Governor Stokes, August 23, 1831, North Carolina Governors' Papers, LXII, *ibid.;* Colonel Charles Spiers to Stokes, August 25, 1831, *ibid.;* Solon Borland to Stokes, September 18, 1831, *ibid.* (see also North Carolina Governors' Letterbooks, 56–57); Order of Hertford County, North Carolina, Court of Pleas, August 1831, *ibid.;* John L. Laughton and E. W. Best to Stokes, August 24, 1831, *ibid.;* Major General M. T. Hawkins to Stokes, August 26, 1831, *ibid.;* Carter Jones to Stokes, August 26, 1831, *ibid.;* Norfolk *Herald,* August 26, 1831, and Baltimore *Niles Register,* September 3, 1831; Drewry, *Southampton Insurrection,* 58, 75–81.

18. Nat's *Confessions* in Tragle, *Southampton Slave Revolt,* 315; Southampton County slave trial records in *ibid.,* 182, 183, 192; Blunt's remarks to Pleasants, Richmond *Whig,* September 3, 1831; unsigned letter from Jerusalem, September 17, 1831, in *ibid.,* September 26, 1831; unsigned letter from Jerusalem, August 24, 1831, in Richmond *Enquirer,* August 30, 1831; unsigned letter from Jerusalem, August 31, in Richmond *Compiler,* September 3, 1831; Drewry, *Southampton Insurrection,* 70–72. The newspaper accounts cited above testified to the loyalty of Blunt's slaves. Significantly, not one of them was ever arrested and tried for participation in the revolt.

19. Last skirmish at the Harris plantation, scenes at Cross Keys, and Nat in hiding: Nat's *Confessions* in Tragle, *Southampton Slave Revolt,* 315; Southampton County slave trial records in *ibid.,* 186–188; Nat's court interrogation on October 31, 1831, as reported in unsigned letter from Jerusalem, October 31, 1831, in Richmond *Whig,* November 7, 1831; Drewry, *Southampton Insurrection,* 48–49, 54, 73, 74, 85.

20. Troops in Southampton and the end of the revolt: Pleasants's report from Jerusalem, August 25 and 27, 1831, in Richmond *Whig,* August 29, 1831; unsigned letter from Jerusalem, August 24, 1831, in Richmond *Enquirer,* August 30, 1831; unsigned letter from Jerusalem, August 27, in Norfolk *American Beacon,* August 30, 1831; Benjamin Eppes's letter from Jerusalem, August 24, 1831, in Richmond *Compiler,* August 27, 1831; memorandum of a North Carolina militiaman, August 23, 1831, North Carolina Governors' Papers, LXII, North Carolina Department of Archives. Capture and execution of bona fide rebels: Pleasants's report ("high pitch of rage") from Jerusalem, August 25 and 27, 1831, in Richmond *Whig,* August 29, 1831, and Pleasants's account in *ibid.,* September 3, 1831; Floyd to Hamilton, November 19, 1831, Floyd Papers, Library of Congress; E. P. Guion to Thomas Ruffin, August 28, 1831, *Papers of Thomas Ruffin* (ed. by J. G. de Roulhac Hamilton, 4 vols., Raleigh, N.C., 1918–1920), II, 45; Southampton County slave trial records in Tragle, *Southampton Slave Revolt,* 181, 194–195, 196, 203–204, 218, 227; Floyd's Diary, September 1 and 2, 1831, Archives of the Virginia State Library; Norfolk *American Beacon,* August 29 and 30, September 9, 1831; Eppes's letter from Jerusalem, August 24, 1831, in Richmond *Compiler,* August 27, 1831; Fayetteville (N.C.) *Journal,* August 27, 29, 31, 1831; memorandum of a North Carolina militiaman, North Carolina Governors' Papers, LXII, North Carolina Department of Archives; Drewry, *Southampton Insurrection,* 72n, 84–88, 96.

21. Pleasant's report from Jerusalem, August 25 and 27, 1831, in Richmond *Whig,* August 29, 1831, and Pleasants's account in *ibid.,* September 3, 1831; Norfolk *American Beacon,* September 6, 1831, as cited in Tragle, *Southampton Slave Revolt,* 400; Cromwell, "Aftermath of Nat Turner's Insurrection," *Journal of Negro History,* V, 212; Norfolk *Herald,* August 26, 1831; Roanoke *Advocate,* October 12, 1831; *North Carolina Journal,* August 27, 1831; Robert Parker to Rebecca Maney, August 29, 1831, as cited in Johnson, *Nat Turner Insurrection,* 113–114; memorandum of a North Carolina militiaman, August 23, 1831, North Carolina Governors' Papers, LXII, North Carolina Department of Archives; Spiers to Stokes, August 25, 1831, *ibid.;* Solon Borland to R. Borland, August 31, 1831, and to Stokes,

September 18, 1831, *ibid.;* S. Whitaker to Stokes, August 26, 1831, *ibid.;* Capehart to Nicholls, August 23–26, Nicholls Papers, *ibid.;* Edenton (N.C.) *Gazette,* September 22, 1831; Huntsville, Alabama, *Southern Advocate,* October 15, 1831; unsigned letter from Jerusalem, September 17, 1831, in Richmond *Whig,* September 26, 1831; Tragle, *Southampton Slave Revolt,* 397; Drewry, *Southampton Insurrection,* 85; Higginson, "Nat Turner's Insurrection," *Black Rebellion,* 185–190.

22. Eppes's proclamation of August 28, 1831, in Lynchburg *Virginian,* September 8, 1831; Richmond *Whig,* August 29, 1831; Norfolk *American Beacon,* September 3, 1831; Floyd to Eppes, September 10, 1831, Virginia Governors' Letterbooks, Archives of the Virginia State Library; Floyd's Diary, September 4, 1831, *ibid.;* Baltimore *Niles Register,* September 3, 1831; Jerusalem citizens to Andrew Jackson in Drewry, *Southampton Insurrection,* 84–85; unsigned letter from Jerusalem, August 24, 1831, in Richmond *Enquirer,* August 30, 1831; unsigned letter from Jerusalem, September 17, 1831, in Richmond *Whig,* September 24, 1831; and Pleasants's account in *ibid.,* September 3, 1831.

23. Pleasants's report from Jerusalem, August 25 and 27, 1831, in Richmond *Whig,* August 29, 1831, and Pleasants's account in *ibid.,* September 3, 1831; unsigned letter from Jerusalem, September 17, 1831, in *ibid.,* September 26, 1831; Richmond *Compiler,* August 27, 1831; unsigned letter from Jerusalem, August 31, 1831, in *ibid.,* September 3, 1831; unsigned letters from Jerusalem, August 24 and September 21, 1831, in Richmond *Enquirer,* August 30 and September 27, 1831.

24. Tragle, *Southampton Slave Revolt,* 173–245, 402; unsigned letter from Jerusalem, September 17, 1831, in Richmond *Whig,* September 26, 1831; unsigned letter from Jerusalem (the author was involved in trying "these scoundrels"), September 4, 1831, in *ibid.,* September 8, 1831; T. Trezevant's letter from Jerusalem ("we commence hanging"), September 3 and 4, 1831, in *ibid.;* William Parker to Bernard Peyton, September 14, 1831, Virginia Governors' Papers, Archives of the Virginia State Library; Floyd's Diary, September 3, 5, 10, and 16, 1831, *ibid.;* Floyd to Eppes, September 6, 1831, Virginia Governors' Letterbooks, *ibid.;* Floyd's instructions to the court clerks in Southampton, Nansemond, Isle of Wight, Sussex, and Prince George counties, September 26, 1831, *ibid.;* U.S. Census Returns for 1830, Southampton County, Virginia; Drewry, *Southampton Insurrection,* 59, 87–88, 95.

25. Joseph C. Robert, *Road to Monticello: A Study of the Virginia Slave Debate of 1832* (Durham, N.C., 1941), 17–18; Rachel Lararuz to Geo. W. Mordecai, October 6, 1831, Pattie Mordecai Papers, North Carolina Department of Archives; Mrs. Lawrence Lewis to Harrison Gray

Otis, October 17, 1831, in Samuel Eliot Morison, *Life and Letters of Harrison Gray Otis* (2 vols., Boston and New York, 1913), II, 260.

26. Aptheker, *American Negro Slave Revolts,* 311; Freehling, *Prelude to Civil War,* 63; Hamilton to Stokes, November 14, 1831, North Carolina Governors' Letterbooks, 70, North Carolina Department of Archives.

27. Borland to R. Borland, August 31, 1831, and Borland to Stokes, September 18, 1831, North Carolina Governors' Papers, LXII, North Carolina Department of Archives; citizens of Scotland Neck, Halifax County, to Stokes, September 22, 1831, *ibid.;* Ben Watson of Hyde County to Stokes, September 25, 1831, and Thos. Singleton of Hyde County to Stokes, September 21, 1831, *ibid.;* citizens of Louisburg, N.C., to Stokes, September 15, 1831, *ibid.;* J. H. Simms of Halifax County to Stokes, September 16, 1831, *ibid.;* William P. Taylor and others to Stokes, October, 1831, North Carolina Governors' Letterbooks, 63, *ibid.;* Norfolk *American Beacon,* August 27, 1831; Drewry, *Southampton Insurrection,* 80, 155.

28. Major-General Nathan B. Whitfield to Stokes, September 12 and 14, 1831, North Carolina Governors' Papers, LXII, North Carolina Department of Archives; William Blanks and others to Stokes, September 13, 1831, *ibid.;* J. M. Gregory to Stokes, September 17, 1831, and Carter Jones to Stokes, September 17, 1831, *ibid.;* citizens' committee of Wilmington to Stokes, September 14, 1831, *ibid.;* Emma Mordecai to Ellen Mordecai, September 16, 1831, Pattie Mordecai Papers, *ibid.;* Raleigh *Star,* September 15, 16, and 22, 1831; Raleigh *Register,* September 15 and 22, 1831; Baltimore *Niles Register,* September 24, 1831; Robert N. Elliott, "The Nat Turner Insurrection as Reported in the North Carolina Press," *North Carolina Historical Review,* XXXVIII (January, 1961), 1–18.

29. Stokes to Hamilton, November 18, 1831, North Carolina Governors' Letterbooks, 70–71, North Carolina Department of Archives; Stokes's Message to the Legislature, November 22, 1831, *ibid.,* 81–87.

30. Floyd's Diary, August 25–30, 1831, and *passim,* Archives of the Virginia State Library. Floyd's Governor's Papers abound in distress calls, reports of slave risings, and pleas for help. See for example the letters to him from Colonel Thos. Spencer of King and Queen County, September 24, 1831; from Wm. Christian of Northampton County, September 1, 1831; from A. Dupuy of Prince Edward County, September 19, 1831; from Brigadier-General Benj. Cabell [?] of Danville, September 20, 1831; from Captain Peter Baird of Prince George County, September 11, 1831; from J. Gibson of Culpeper Court House, September 19, 1831; from N. Sutton of Bowling Green, September 21,

1831; from a citizen of Leesburg, September 18, 1831; from David G. Garlands of Amherst County, October 6, 1831; from the citizens of Westmoreland County, October 3, 1831; from Captain Robert Hill of Madison Court House, September 2, 1831; from R. M. Patterson and students of the University of Virginia, November 3, 1831; and from citizens of Chesterfield County [September 1831]. Quotation (*"panic* in all the country") in a letter a Virginian sent to an Ohio acquaintance, published in the Cincinnati *Journal* and reprinted in the *Liberator,* January 28, 1832. On Floyd's reaction to the distress calls, see Richmond *Enquirer,* September 2, 1831; Floyd's Diary, entries for September and October, 1831, Archives of the Virginia State Library; Floyd to Colonel William Christian, September 7, 1831, Virginia Executive Letterbooks; and Floyd to John W. Cole, August 25, 1831, to William H. Broadnax, August 29, 1831, and to Eppes, August 31 and September 6, 1831, *ibid.*

31. Richmond *Whig,* September 3 and 26, 1831.

32. Floyd's Diary, September 3, 5, 10, 16, 19, 20, 26, 27, and October 13 and 17, 1831, Archives of the Virginia State Library; Floyd to John Crump, September 1, 1831, and Floyd to Colonel J. Holiday, Virginia Executive Letterbooks, *ibid.;* Floyd to Mayor John E. Holt of Norfolk, August 31, 1831, and to Colonel W. J. Worth of the 2nd U.S. Artillery at Norfolk, September 2, 1831, *ibid.;* and Floyd's Free Negro and Slave Letterbook, *ibid.*

33. Richmond *Whig,* September 26, 1831.

34. On the rewards for Nat: Floyd to Eppes, September 13, 1831, Virginia Executive Letterbooks, Archives of the Virginia State Library; Parker to Floyd, September 14, 1831, Virginia Executive Communications, *ibid.;* Floyd's proclamation of reward, September 17, 1831, in Richmond *Enquirer,* September 27, 1831, and in Tragle, *Southampton Slave Revolt,* 421–423; Higginson, "Nat Turner's Insurrection," *Black Rebellion,* 202. Rumors of Nat's whereabouts in Fredericksburg *Virginia Herald,* September 7, 1831; Fincastle *Patriot,* September 30, 1831, as quoted in Richmond *Enquirer,* October 7, 1831; Drewry, *Southampton Insurrection,* 89.

35. Nat in hiding: Nat's *Confessions* in Tragle, *Southampton Slave Revolt,* 315–316; Nat's court interrogation of October 31, 1831, as reported in unsigned letter from Jerusalem, October 31, 1831, in Richmond *Whig,* November 7, 1831, and in unsigned letter from Southampton, November 1, 1831, in Richmond *Enquirer,* November 8, 1831; *ibid.,* October 25, 1831; letter from Elliot Whitehead of Suffolk in *ibid.,* November 15, 1831; Higginson, "Nat Turner's Insurrection," *Black Rebellion,* 202–206; and Drewry, *Southampton Insurrection,*

90–92. Nat's capture: Nat's *Confessions* in Tragle, *Southampton Slave Revolt*, 303, 316; Richmond *Enquirer*, November 15, 1831; unsigned letter from Southampton, November 1, 1831, in *ibid.*, November 8, 1831; unsigned letter from Jerusalem, October 31, 1831, in Richmond *Whig*, November 7, 1831; Norfolk *Herald*, November 4, 1831; Drewry, *Southampton Insurrection*, 92–93.

36. Drewry, *Southampton Insurrection*, 91n, 93–94; ("a mere scarecrow") from Higginson, "Nat Turner's Insurrection," *Black Rebellion*, 205; Richmond *Enquirer*, November 4, 1831; Petersburg *Intelligencer*, November 4, 1831; Norfolk *Herald*, November 4, 1831.

37. Nat's court interrogation of October 31, 1831, as reported in his trial, Tragle, *Southampton Slave Revolt*, 222; in T. Trezevant's letter of October 31 in Norfolk *American Beacon*, November 2, 1831; in unsigned letter from Jerusalem, October 31, 1831, in Richmond *Whig*, November 7, 1831; and in unsigned letter from Southampton, November 1, 1831, in Richmond *Enquirer*, November 8, 1831; Drewry, *Southampton Insurrection*, 91, 117.

38. Tragle, *Southampton Slave Revolt*, 302–321, contains the entire *Confessions*, including Gray's introduction and epilogue.

39. Among those who have questioned the authenticity of the *Confessions* are Tragle, *Southampton Slave Revolt*, 403, 409, and Gross and Bender, "History, Politics, and Literature," *American Quarterly*, XXVIII, 487–518.

40. Foner, *Nat Turner*, 37, also regards the *Confessions* as authentic. One should note, though, that the summary of Nat's trial, which Gray appended to his epilogue, contains a speech by Judge Cobb considerably more dramatic than the prosaic remarks in the actual transcript. I stayed with the prosaic remarks.

41. Southampton County slave trial records in Tragle, *Southampton Slave Revolt*, 221–223, 227, and *ibid.*, 169, 406n; Nat's *Confessions* in *ibid.*, 318; Petersburg *Intelligencer* as quoted in Richmond *Enquirer*, November 22, 1831; Rokela, "A Page in History—One of the Tragedies of the Old Slavery Days," *Godey's Magazine* CXXXVI (March, 1898), 292; and Drewry, *Southampton Insurrection*, 98–102.

42. Southampton County slave trial records in Tragle, *Southampton Slave Revolt*, 223, 227; Southampton County Superior Court Orders (1832), IV, 21, 28; slave trial records in the Court Order Books of Sussex, Isle of Wight, and Surry counties; Floyd's Diary, September 16, 1831, Archives of the Virginia State Library; Floyd to Macon County magistrate, October 13, 1831, Virginia Executive Letterbooks, *ibid.*; M. Daniel of Sussex County to Floyd, September 15, 1831, Virginia Governors' Papers, *ibid.*; Richmond *Whig*, September 19, 1831; Lucy Mae

Turner, "Family of Nat Turner," *Negro History Bulletin,* XVIII, 127–132, 155–158; and Tragle's taped interview with Herbert Turner of Boykins, Virginia, May 12, 1969, as cited in *Southampton Slave Revolt,* 13. For descriptions of slave trials and hangings in other counties, see Johnson, *Nat Turner Insurrection,* 127–129, and Drewry, *Southampton Insurrection,* 86–87, 111, 115.

PART FOUR: LEGACY

1. Richmond *Enquirer,* September 27, 1831; Postmaster J. C. Harris of Orange County, Virginia, to Floyd, September 25, 1831, Floyd's Free Negro and Slave Letterbook, Archives of the Virginia State Library; Floyd to Harris, September 27, 1831, Virginia Governors' Letterbooks, *ibid.;* plus sources cited in notes 2 and 4 below.
2. Floyd to Hamilton, Floyd Papers, Library of Congress; Floyd to Eppes, September 6, 1831, Virginia Governors' Papers, Archives of the Virginia State Library; Floyd to Harris, September 27, 1831, Floyd's Free Negro and Slave Letterbook, *ibid.;* Floyd's Diary, September 9 and 27, October 11, 16, 18, and 20, 1831, *ibid.* See the items collected in Floyd's Free Negro and Slave Letterbook, including eleven copies of the *Liberator,* ranging in dates from May 7 to October 15, 1831; Sherlock Gregory of Albany to Postmaster of Chancellorsville, Virginia, September 10, 1831; "Nero" of Boston ("Nero" was evidently black) to the Jerusalem Postmaster [n. d.]; "L. N. Q." of Philadelphia to Floyd, October 15, 1831, and "L. N. Z." of Philadelphia to Floyd, October 24, 1831. On October 20, Floyd answered "L. N. Q." and copied the letter into his Diary on the same day. See also N. Sutton to Floyd, September 21, 1831, Virginia Governors' Papers, *ibid.;* Brigadier-General George Cooke to Floyd, September 13, 1831, *ibid.;* "A Friend to the city" of Richmond to Floyd [November 1831], *ibid.*
3. For Northern reactions to the rebellion, consult Foner, *Nat Turner,* 75–79; Boston *Statesman* as quoted in the Alexandria, Va., *Gazette,* September, 1831 (and printed in Tragle, *Southampton Slave Revolt,* 88–89); and the *Liberator* (quoting other Northern papers), September 17 and October 1, 1831.
4. See, for example, Richmond *Enquirer,* September 27, 1831; New York *Daily Sentinel,* October 11, 1831; Raleigh *Register,* September 16 and 22, October 13, 1831; Baltimore *Niles Register,* October 29, 1831; Fayetteville, N.C., *Carolina Observer,* September 21, 1831; Washington *National Intelligencer* as quoted in *ibid.,* and in Raleigh *Register,* September 22, 1831, and in Raleigh *Star,* September 29, 1831; Mrs. Lewis to Otis, October 17, 1831, in Morison, *Otis,* II, 260; *Liberator,*

September 3 and October 1, 1831; Freehling, *Prelude to Civil War,* 63; Aptheker, *American Negro Slave Revolts,* 111; Foner, *Nat Turner,* 7, 87; and Tragle, *Southampton Slave Revolt,* 152.

5. Cromwell, "Aftermath of Nat Turner's Insurrection," *Journal of Negro History,* 208–234; Richmond *Whig,* September 29, October 13 and 17, November 21, 1831, and January 21, 1832 (containing Pleasants's editorial in favor of gradual abolition); Richmond *Enquirer,* November 11, 1831, and February 4, 1832.

6. Floyd's Diary, October 10 and 24, November 10, 21, and 28, December 1, 3, 4, 6, and 29, 1831, Archives of the Virginia State Library; Floyd to Hamilton, November 19, 1831, Floyd Papers, Library of Congress; Ambler, *Life and Diary of Floyd,* 91–92.

7. Floyd's Message to the Legislature, December 6, 1831, in Journal of the House of Delegates, Archives of the Virginia State Library (and printed in Tragle, *Southampton Slave Revolt,* 430–444). On December 31, 1831, Floyd sent to the House of Delegates "all the papers in relation to the insurrection in Southampton," which had been filed together in a special bundle. This mysterious bundle has never been located.

8. Richmond *Enquirer,* February 4, 1832, and *passim;* Richmond *Whig* (which also published the debates), issues from January through March, 1832; Cromwell, "Aftermath of Nat Turner's Insurrection," *Journal of Negro History,* 208–234; Foner, *Nat Turner,* 99–116; and Robert, *Road to Monticello.* On December 26, before the debate began, Governor Floyd confided in his Diary that a discussion of slavery "must come if I can influence my friends in the Assembly to bring it on. I will not rest until slavery is abolished in Virginia." Yet, from all appearances, he did little if anything to get it abolished. When the debate opened Floyd "seemed to function strictly as an observer" (Tragle, *Southampton Slave Revolt,* 250) and even doubted the wisdom of the debates when they became acrimonious (Diary entries of January 21 and 24, 1832).

9. Ambler, *Life and Diary of Floyd,* 91–92; George M. Fredrickson, *The Black Image in the White Mind: The Debate on Afro-American Character and Destiny, 1817–1914* (New York, 1971), 44–46; abridged version of Dew's essay in Harvey Wish (ed.), *Slavery in the South* (New York, 1964), 234–251.

10. My summary of the Southern reaction derives from many studies, among them, Freehling, *Prelude to Civil War,* 301–360; Franklin, *Militant South,* 63–95; Clement Eaton, *Freedom-of-Thought Struggle in the Old South* (revised and enlarged ed., New York, 1964), 89ff; Lloyd, *Slavery Controversy,* 49ff; William S. Jenkins, *Pro-Slavery*

Thought in the Old South (Chapel Hill, N.C., 1935); Fredrickson, *Black Image in the White Mind,* 46–70; Sydnor, *Development of Southern Sectionalism,* 222–248; Sellers, "Travail of Slavery," *Southerner as American,* 40–71; W. J. Cash, *Mind of the South* (New York, 1941), Book One; and Eugene D. Genovese, *Political Economy of Slavery* (paperback ed., New York, 1967). I am not, of course, contending that the Old South became a monolithic slave dictatorship. On the contrary, there were dissenters in Dixie and liberating cracks in the Southern slave regime down to the Civil War, as scholars like Carl N. Degler and Richard C. Wade have demonstrated. See Degler, *The Other South: Southern Dissenters in the Nineteenth Century* (New York, 1974), 13–157, and Wade, *Slavery in the Cities* (New York, 1964). Nevertheless, from the point of view of slave discipline and control, the Southern slave system was so repressive that no more rebellions broke out after the 1830s.

11. My interview with Gilbert Francis, Boykins, Virginia, July 16, 1973.

12. Warner pamphlet in Tragle, *Southampton Slave Revolt,* 281–300.

13. Richmond *Enquirer,* December 2, 1831; Higginson, "Nat Turner's Insurrection," *Black Rebellion,* 207; Tragle, *Southampton Slave Revolt,* 279, 327, 346; Foner, *Nat Turner,* 37; Drewry, *Southampton Insurrection,* 169n; Gross and Bender, "History, Politics, and Literature," *American Quarterly,* XXIII, 500.

14. Drewry, *Southampton Insurrection,* 179–180; Higginson, "Nat Turner's Insurrection," *Black Rebellion,* 214. In a ringing speech during the Virginia slave debates of 1832, James McDowell declared that what distressed Southern whites so was "the suspicion eternally attached to the slave himself, the suspicion that a Nat Turner might be in every family, that the same bloody deed could be acted over at any time and in any place, that the materials for it were spread through the land and always ready for a like explosion. . . ." McDowell's speech in Foner, *Nat Turner,* 112–113. According to Drewry and F. Roy Johnson (*Nat Turner Story,* 214–215), rumors of "nigger uprisings" continued to haunt whites in southeastern Virginia as late as the 1890s.

15. Percy Claud of Boykins, Virginia, to Henry Tragle, April 24, 1969, in Tragle, *Southampton Slave Revolt,* 13. See also *ibid.,* 12–13, and Johnson, *Nat Turner Story,* 179–213.

INDEX

Petersburg (Virginia): militia, 47
  slave unrest, 49
  Turner rebellion, 91
Phipps, Benjamin, 116–17
Pleasants, John Hampden, 92
  emancipation endorsed, 136
  Turner rebellion, 82, 97–98, 109–
    10, 113
    theory of Nat's religious fana-
      ticism, 101–02, 113
  see also Richmond Whig
Porter, Henry (slave): Turner rebel-
    lion, 52, 53, 55, 66, 81, 98,
    120
Porter, Richard, 52, 76, 77
Porter, Venus (slave), 77
Porter family, 38
Prosser, Gabriel: conspiracy, 16–17,
    18, 19, 42

Quakers: antislavery, 9, 17, 45, 112

Raleigh (North Carolina): Turner
    rebellion and aftermath, 107–
    08
Raleigh Register, 108
Raleigh Star, 108
Randolph, John, 17
Reese, Cherry (slave; Nat's wife),
    29, 126
  and Nat, 29, 30, 32, 39, 53
    children, 30, 39, 69, 97, 126
    Nat's papers entrusted to, 69,
      102
Reese, Giles, 30, 39, 69, 88
Reese, Jack (slave), 66–67
  Turner rebellion, 66, 67, 68, 70,
    71, 99, 120
Reese, John, 65
Reese, Mrs. Piety, 71
Reese, William, 66, 71
rice, 44, 46
Richie, Thomas, 139
Richmond (Virginia): militia, 47,
    50
  Prosser conspiracy, 16–17, 18, 19,
    42

slave unrest, 15, 16–18
Turner rebellion and aftermath,
    91–93, 109
Richmond Compiler, 92
Richmond Enquirer: Garrison and
    the Liberator, 134
  slavery debates, 139
  Turner rebellion, 101
    Confessions, 145
    Nat's interrogation, 118, 119–20
Richmond Whig: emancipation en-
    dorsed, 136
  Turner rebellion, 92, 97-98, 109-
    10, 112–13
    Nat's interrogation, 118
    Nat's papers, 102
    trials, 104
Ridley, Curtis (slave), 95–96
Ridley, Stephen (slave), 95–96
Ridley, Thomas, 2, 90, 94, 104

Santo Domingo, 11
  slave rebellion, 11, 15–16, 18, 42,
    48
slavery: codes made more severe
    (1832–33), 140, 141, 142,
    144
  Calhoun's justification for, 143
  Dew's justification for, 140–41,
    143
  economic justification for, 19
  education for slaves, 48, 131, 140,
    141
  family life, 23, 24
  grapevine, 16, 17, 23, 29, 47, 51,
    82
  historical justification for, 19, 141,
    143
  Missouri Compromise (and de-
    bates), 42, 45
  racist justification for, 10, 41, 143,
    144
  religion and slave church, 3, 16,
    25–26, 37, 52, 56, 109, 112,
    131–32, 138, 140, 141

184

ABOUT THE AUTHOR

Prize-winning biographer Stephen B. Oates has published thirteen books and more than seventy articles. He is especially acclaimed for his Civil War Quartet, which comprises *To Purge This Land with Blood: A Biography of John Brown* (1970, 1984), *The Fires of Jubilee* (1975), *With Malice Toward None: The Life of Abraham Lincoln* (1977), and *Let the Trumpet Sound: The Life of Martin Luther King, Jr.* (1982). *With Malice Toward None*, hailed as the best one-volume life of Lincoln, won a Christopher Award and the Barondess/Lincoln Award of the New York Civil War Round Table. *Let the Trumpet Sound* also won a Christopher Award plus the Robert F. Kennedy Memorial Book Award. The two volumes have also appeared in several foreign languages. Mr. Oates' other books include *Rip Ford's Texas* (1963, 1987), *Our Fiery Trial: John Brown, Abraham Lincoln, and the Civil War Era* (1979), *Abraham Lincoln: The Man Behind the Myths* (1984), *Portrait of America* (2 vols., 1986), *Biography as High Adventure* (1986), and *William Faulkner: The Man and the Artist* (1987), to be translated into French, German, Spanish, and Portuguese editions. Mr. Oates is currently Professor of History and Paul Murray Kendall Professor of Biography at the Univesity of Massachusetts, Amherst.